T0148186

I David

Anatomy of an Adopted Child

David J. Lamb

   www.trafford.com

North America & international
toll-free: 1 888 232 4444 (USA & Canada)
phone: 250 383 6864 ♦ fax: 812 355 4082

CONTENTS

ACKNOWLEDGMENT

I'm devoting this book to my dear wife who encouraged me to write about my life. Through her devotion, love and insistence I was able to complete this task. I have been putting this off for years.

PREFACE

T his is a book about my life as a young boy being adopted from an orphanage when I was 4 1/2 years old. The people adopting me were not prepared to have a child. There were many trials and tribulations during the years I was with my adopted parents.

I was adopted by a couple who thought their marriage would be repaired if they were to bring a young child into their family. Not expecting the kind of difficulties they would have with a high-energy child, when they tried to communicate with this child they were unable to resolve issues in child behavior.

Consequently the rearing of this child became a matter of discipline of unexpected proportions. Not only were they short of techniques, but also ignorant of the emotional instability they created in the child through harsh punishment and demands.

The adopted parents were never sympathetic to the emotional needs of this young boy they brought into their family. In an attempt to have the perfect child they complicated and exacerbated the opposite effect on this child's behavior he exhibited.

To be taken from the orphanage environment and placed into a single-family situation was very traumatic. Confusion and uncertainty caused this little boy to react in negative ways.

This book attempts to portray a blow-by-blow account of the difficulties this child had with his adopted parents. The book also includes how he was able to find solace in his everyday struggles.

Only through stubbornness was he able to overcome the lack of understanding of his adopted parents. He eventually grew to accomplish success.

Through this book I hope that you will understand the significance of an adoption and what impact it has on a child.

CHAPTER 1

THE BEGINNING

I t is said that all men are created equal, however this is not always true. Some mothers abandoned their babies, giving them away, placing them in foster care, or sending them to an orphanage. In my case the latter happened, I was placed in an orphanage. It is my understanding that I was placed in an orphanage because my mother could not afford me. She was living on a meager income working in a school cafeteria in Aurora, Illinois.

At the time of my birth she already had seven children, two of the children had already been placed in the orphanage before me. Mother really did not have any other alternative but to put me up for adoption. I was born out of wedlock, which would've made it difficult for my mother. I resided in the orphanage four and one-half years. My mother worked for the Servite Fathers prior to my birth. She worked for the Servite Fathers to help pay for my birth.

My mother Mary Susanna May, was born in Aurora, Illinois February 22, 1905. Mother attended the nearby Catholic school, St. Joseph's Catholic School. The Teachers were from the order of St. Francis Sisters of Milwaukee. They coaxed mother into joining their Order. Fate changed her role in life. She went to a dance one evening and met Paul Edward Manning. As time progressed they became very close. Paul's parents invited Mary and her father to move in with them. On January 17, 1922 Mary and Paul were married at Sacred Hearts Church in Aurora, Illinois. Before her husband passed away, they had five children: Tim Manning-September 5, 1922, Mary Manning-June 17, 1924, Peter Manning—January 24, 1926, Patti Manning—February 22, 1928 and Dan Manning—August 4, 1930.

My mother's mother died giving birth to her second child. My mother was 2 years old. She was raised by her father. My mother's father, Dominick was a house painter. He spent a great deal of time in taverns. I was told my mother would go to the tavern with him and sit on the barstool. Much of her young life was spent in taverns. I am sure this type of childhood life had an influence on her adult life. She became an alcoholic. She was a very friendly person, and along with her drinking, she was very vulnerable with men.

The children's father contracted Tuberculosis in May 1926 and spent the better part of seven years in Springbrook Sanitarium in Aurora. He was allowed to come home for a few weeks every year but the children were never allowed in his bedroom.

While in the sanitarium, her husband built a HAM radio transmitter. The United States Radio Commission issued him an amateur radio station license. His call letters were W9GKX. Upon completion of the radio transmitter, he brought it with him whenever he was able to visit his home. Mother would call "HAM" radio operators around the world and make friends. The children's father passed away from chronic pulmonary TB May 31, 1933. He was only 31 years old.

In 1934 mother went to work and lived with Ray Travis in Aurora. It was at this time my mother became pregnant with my sister Nanette out of wedlock.

In 1936 Mary was back living with the Manning's. During this time she began dating their "Egg Man" Fred Kruhman. My sister Mary always called the man delivering eggs the "Egg Man." My brother Frank was conceived in this relationship. My sister Mary said, "mother would always get on her best dress, when she knew the "Egg Man" was coming".

On September 17, 1938 I was born. My name now is David Joseph Lamb. My birth name was Joseph David Sharp. My birth father's name is George Sharp who lived in Chicago, Illinois and work as an elevator engineer. He was much older than my mother and passed away at the age of 96.

The three fathers abandoned Mary without giving her any support in raising these children. Frank, Nanette and I were the only ones placed in the orphanage.

Nanette did not know that she was adopted until her adopted parents passed away. She discovered by going through the personal papers of her parents, that she was adopted. She became so upset, that she threw the adoption papers away. It wasn't until I contacted her on her 70th birthday that she remembered throwing the adoption papers away. Like me she didn't know until this time that she had other brothers and sisters.

Mary had no funds to raise these children, so with the help of Father Charles Kelly, Pastor of St. Mary's Church in Aurora these three children were placed in St. Vincent's orphanage. I was told that my mother went into seclusion for six months each time she got pregnant. During the 30s and 40s pregnancies out of wedlock were kept secret. Women having babies without being married were considered trash. To help pay for my birth she worked for the Servite Fathers. Mother never let the Manning children know about the births of the other children.

In May 1941, my mother married Harry Redfield in Urbana, Illinois. On September 21, 1942 they had a son who they named Barry Redfield. Barry was born in Rockham, South Dakota. My mother and Barry's dad lived in Rockham working as cooks for the Burlington Railroad. My brother told me that they lived out of a boxcar on the train and all he had to play with was a Shepherd dog. Barry never saw another child until he was six years old.

My mother had another child. A baby girl that she claimed died at birth. Because I haven't been able to obtain any information on her, we can only assume she was adopted from the hospital.

It appears as though our mother had a child every two years. Family members have told me, Mother was often intoxicated. Once my brother Tim had to take her home from the Christmas visit. He didn't want his children exposed to her while intoxicated. She suffered from depression. Depression tends to run in the family. During my younger years I too was often depressed. Depression would come on for no reason. I now take medication to stave off depression. One time when I was driving home from college I thought of committing suicide. I had taken an overload of college courses and it was getting to me.

Eventually the five children were taken from my mother and placed with their grandparents. During this time my mother was not allowed to see the children, this must have been very difficult for her. The children became wards of the state. Mother was not allowed to be in contact with the children. My sister Mary told me the bus stopped for school just outside her living room window where she could see the children boarding. This must have been extremely crushing for my mother.

At the age of six Barry was brought to Aurora to stay with his older brother Tim. Barry stayed at Tim's house and our sister Mary provided financial support. He stayed with them throughout high school. After graduating from high school Barry enlisted in the Air Force.

This is a brief history of the early years of my family. I will explain later how I found my family.

I don't remember a lot about the orphanage during my 4 1/2 year residency, but I will try to recall to the best of my knowledge, including additional sources such as newspapers and source documents. I will try to reconstruct my years at the orphanage.

St. Vincent's Orphanage was a multiple story building that housed as many as 300 children during the 40s and 60s. The orphanage was constructed in 1896 and terminated in 1973.

During the years between the 1940s and 1960s it was home to 300 children. An estimated 27,000 children came through St. Vincent's home over the 78 years. St. Vincent's was founded by Rev. Clemens Kavelage and the Sisters of St. Francis of the Sacred Heart, an Order from Mokeena, Illinois. By the early 1970s foster care had replaced institutional care for needy and dependent children and the home closed. For a time after that, the building was converted to a school for the developmentally disabled children.

The demolition of the orphanage was an emotional event for some former residents and employees of the home, as well as for many Freeport citizens who loyally supported the home with their donations for many years.

The orphanage had many large rooms. I recall our bedroom was lined with several rows of large cribs with tall side rails, similar to a baby bed but much larger. Each evening before going to bed we removed our clothes, folded them and place them on the chair next to our bed. Before we went to bed we had to say our evening prayer, I still remember it to this day. There was a prayer to our Guardian Angel and it goes like this:

> Angel of God my guide and dear to whom
> His love permits me here. And every day be
> at my side to love, to rule, to guard and guide.

In the morning when it was time to get up, we were taken to the bathroom where 14 children at a time, could groom themselves at individual sinks each, separated by marble partitions. The Sisters would see that we washed behind the ears and that our neck was scrubbed. Upon completion of our morning bath, we would put on clean clothes and say our morning prayer "The Guardian Angel". Then Sister would march us single file to the cafeteria, without talking.

The cafeteria was also a very large room with rows of tables. When it was time to eat, we all marched single file into the cafeteria and stood by our assigned places. We remained standing until everyone was in the room, then we all sat down together. We were taught to remain quiet while being served and eating. Most of the food was served out of large kettles.

I don't remember, but I think our food was served in a bowl. Most of the food was served with a ladle. I recall the first meal with my adopted parents included meat. I had a great deal of difficulty trying to swallow the meat. I was told I had to clean my plate before leaving the table. It took me until my aunt and mother finished washing the dishes, before I finally swallowed a piece of meat. The reason I mention this tidbit is because I don't believe that we were served solid food. Most of the food was served in stewed form, therefore most of what we ate was soft.

After breakfast we were led into a large room, single file, with several long tables and were given pictures to color. This was our primary activity before recess. I remember looking out large windows and envying the older students walking by going to school in another part of the building.

I spent a lot of time just daydreaming, instead of doing my work, which was supposed to be: coloring and drawing. I really don't know how long this took before we were allowed out for recess. After recess we marched into another large room where we would sit on the floor and a Sister would read us a story before dinner.

She had a small projector with a colored paper film that projected the objects on the wall. As Sister rotated the pictures by slowly turning a knob on top of the projector, she would tell us a story represented by the pictures. Story time was kind of neat. The lights would all be turned off and the room went completely dark. The images projected were of cartoon characters.

After Sister told us a story, it was time to take a nap. After nap—time we were allowed to go outside for recess. We didn't have any equipment to play with. In fact we just played tag on the blacktop. I recall one time the girls had a playhouse equipped with a play stove, ironing board and a bed. The Playhouse looked intriguing to me, so one day I entered and started playing house with the girls. I lied down on the bed as though I was taking a nap. About that time Sister came in and caught me lying there. My punishment was that I had to stay in for the next several days for recess. I had to stay in the small room that had a screen door. While standing by the screen door and watching the children play, I noticed at the top of the basement stairs were Santa Claus boots. I couldn't resist knocking his boots down the stairs. This was my way of getting even.

The reason I didn't like Santa Claus was because he never brought me any presents. I assumed many years later, that the presents must have been from parents who were keeping their children in the orphanage. I never received any presents during the year or any other time. I vividly remember receiving a new drum one Christmas. I was so happy with my new drum, that I didn't hear Sister when she asked everyone to be quiet, so Santa Claus could speak. I was just having a great old-time beating on my new drum. Consequently, the Sister took my drum away. The drum was never returned, so I was left without a toy to play with. I asked Sister if there were any other toys for me to play with. She said, "find someone to share their toy with you". I'm sure most of the other children had the same problem of not receiving gifts, they only had one toy and weren't about to share.

CHAPTER 2

MY NEW LIFE BEGINS

One day while I was in the classroom studying with the other children Sister asked me to come with her. When we left the classroom there were two women standing there, waiting to greet me. Sister introduced me to one of the ladies and said she was going to be my new mother. I wasn't sure what that meant. She explained to me, that I would be going with her to a new home. After some discussion they led me out to her car. I was afraid to get into the car. I had never seen a car before, so I wasn't quite sure what was going to happen. After we got in the car, my adopted mother gave me a translucent yellow plastic comb. Wow, a comb, I was so excited I actually had received something. Unfortunately as we were riding along, the comb slipped between the back of the seat and the cushion. I couldn't retrieve it. Oh well! Here we go again nothing to play with.

When we arrived at my new home in Rockford, Illinois, I was taken into the house and met my new cousin Kyle. He gave me a little toy Scotty dog. I don't think I let go of the dog for two days. During this time I was also introduced to my Aunt Lorraine, Uncle Forrie, my new dad Harry Lamb and Kate, the lady that came with my adopted mother to the orphanage.

I don't believe my new adopted father wanted any children. He never came to the orphanage with my mother to get me. As I discovered many years later, the reason they adopted children was to hold their marriage together. My adopted mother was extremely jealous of other women. My mother thought children would bring them closer together.

Shortly after they got me, they also adopted a little baby girl whom they named Suzie. Dad did spend time with her, but never with me at first. Also living with us at this time was my Aunt Diane, a half sister to my mother. She was in high school at the time and was staying with my parents after her mother died. She stayed with us until entering into nurses training at St. Anthony's in Rockford.

Diane would take me sledding on Willard Avenue near my cousin Kyle's home. We spent a lot of time together playing outside and sliding down hills, and to see who could go the fastest. When we were a little older we would grab the bumper of city buses and slide with our feet, when there was snow. The sliding went great until we hit a bare spot or the bus exceed 40 mph. My cousin Luke hit some cinders one time, and he went flying into a barbed wire fence and shredded his jacket. He was just lucky he didn't get tore up.

My cousin's parents were poor, so during our early years Kyle and I would get the same major Christmas presents. I remember different years. One year we each received a train set and another time a bicycle. Kyle was six months older than me, so he was able to ride his bike much sooner than I could. This frustrated my dad. Kyle could ride and I couldn't. He would say, "You damn dummy". He never understood the difference in abilities, that age makes a difference. He always expected me to be a man. When I couldn't do something he thought I should be able to do, he would let go swearing a string of profanities. I suffered from this verbal abuse all my young life. Kyle being six months older was obviously better coordinated. There were so many times this type of thing occurred. Another time was when I was trying to fly a kite with difficulty. Dad took the kite from me and began flying it himself. When I kept asking him if I could fly it, my insistence made him mad, so he sent me to my room. I spent the next hour or so looking out my bedroom window watching Kyle and my dad flying kites. Dad never did offer to let me fly the kite. He obviously needed a course in child psychology.

My mother wasn't much fun either. Her punishments were severe. One example: she noticed in the kitchen closet black streaks on the walls from me striking matches. Upon discovering that she got a box of wooden matches and lit one. Then she took my right hand and held out my little finger and held the match to it. Approximately two days later my finger turned black and skin came off. Her beatings were also very generous. One of her frequent sayings was, "wait until your dad gets home". She was saying this while striking me. This usually meant another beating with the heel of Dad's shoe, which was full of steel chips from the factory floor or hitting me with what ever else was at hand. I remember one time I threw a tantrum. He decided that was never going to happen again, so he picked up a three-tine pitchfork and went after me. This was in addition to what my mother already had given me. When I got a beating, one was not good enough they both wanted some of the action. Life wasn't much fun with these people.

Mother thought that I had poor posture, so she would have me march round the coffee table like a soldier for one-half hour at a time. Her idea of having a child behave would be considered child abuse today. More than likely child social services would have removed me from the home.

Since Kyle and I were approximately the same age, we had fun playing together along with getting in trouble. We always managed to fight with other kids in the neighborhood. Often times Kyle would start a fight and I would finish it. We did everything from making slingshots and corncob pipes to climbing trees. One day we were climbing this tall pine tree in the neighbor's yard. Kyle started up the tree first. When Kyle was about one third of the way up the tree I began climbing. As I started up the tree I heard the snapping and cracking of branches, it was Kyle on his way down. He went by me like a rocket all the way to the ground. I climbed back down and at the foot of the tree laid Kyle crying. I couldn't keep myself from laughing. "It's not funny, David" he exclaimed. Then he got up and went home. This was one of many crises we had over the years. When playing Tarzan, we would jump from one roof to a building with a lower roof. This little activity was fun, until one day we went through the roof of the lower building. Wow! Did that ever make my dad mad when he found out! Guess, what I got. Kyle was climbing out of the barn window and fell about 20feet. He was hanging on to a rope and lost his grip. The window was at the peak of the barn. He landed in a feed bunk below. He was lucky no bones were broken. This was the same rope I used to pull the hay up into the barn. We used the hay rope suspended from the ceiling of the haymow to pretend we were swinging from building to building like Tarzan. I don't know what possessed Kyle to grab that part of the rope hanging just outside the window. I guess he planned to shinny down. When he grabbed the rope he discovered it wasn't fastened on the other end.

Kyle also had a younger brother Luke who unfortunately, was always the one who was it, when we play tag or hide and go seek. Luke being younger was quite gullible. I remember one time when we had Luke pee on an electric fence. I recall him jumping back about 6 feet and letting loose with a string of colorful words. Kyle and I thought his distress was funny. One other time we bent over a young Maple tree and had him get on it and then we let go. Luke went sailing through the air. He definitely was our amusement. Later on we got on the trees ourselves, it turned out to be lots of fun.

Well, I suppose like all children, if our parents had known all those things we did as children, we probably wouldn't be living today.

My dad was an Englishman with a very short temper. Consequently I was usually on the end of his belt, shoe or fist. He would use the heel of his shoe full of steel chips picked up from the factory floor. These chips were quite sharp. They were from the metal turnings from a lathe. Dad was a type of man that always needed someone with him. When working on his model "A" Ford truck at night after supper, regardless of the weather, I had to go out and hold a flashlight. This was a very trying experience for me because it never seemed as though I had the flashlight shining where he wanted it. In the first place, I was so damn cold I couldn't hold it still. A number of expletives would come rolling out of his mouth when the light wasn't exactly where he wanted it.

You know as a kid you always want to go with your dad when he takes the car to town. We were walking downtown one day and I was tripping over the cracks in the sidewalk. This was the first time I had ever walked on a sidewalk. I had difficulty negotiating the expansion joints in the concrete. He would look down at me and say, "Pick up your God damn feet". He never knew how to be kind to me or treat me with respect. He always spoke to me harshly and treated me as though I was a grown-up. Dad bought me a pony when I was proximately 5 1/2 years old and expected me to ride it. The pony had never been trained to ride. In fact she never did get trained. Over the years while on the farm I was the only one who could actually ride her and stay on. Many people tried but were thrown off by sudden stops or she would rub against the fence. I never used a saddle I always rode her bareback.

My horse Jill became my close friend on the farm. I used to keep her in the barnyard. During the summer evenings the cows were allowed to go up to the woods. I discovered she could smell the cows and take me right to them. Prior to this I would spend considerable time in the morning trying to locate them for milking. We had 35 acres of dense second growth trees making the cows difficult to find.

My dad was never any fun to go with. He always wanted to take me fishing. When I did go with him and catch a fish, I would ask him if I should keep it. He would tell me, "Hell no, it's too small". Then another time I would catch a fish the same size and ask the same question the response might be "Hell yes". Therefore I was always uneasy trying to guess what his response would be. I never really liked fishing when I was younger. He always insisted that I walked down to the creek with him.

Another experience I had with my dad was when he brought home wood patterns from the factory. This was his primary reason for getting a truck. Then he could haul patterns home from the factory to take apart. Many evenings after work, I had to go outside with him and help take the patterns apart. My job the next day, if not sooner, was to pull out all of the nails, then straighten them, and properly stack the lumber. Over several weeks I pulled out and straightened approximately 22 gallons of nails. My dad was cheap. He intended to reuse the nails, which we did for several years.

The lumber was random width and length. My dad was always trying to find the cheap way of doing things. Rather than buy new lumber he planned on using the lumber for whatever. The lumber had to be taken to the house basement. To do this he used my new wooden wagon. During WWII everything being built for domestic use was made out of wood. My wagon was completely made out of wood, including the wheels. One time when hauling the boards to the basement he broke the wheels, so much for my wagon! Another time he bought me a hammer, which he later broke the handle on trying to pull out a large nail, rather then use a crow bar. My dad never did replace my hammer or wagon. I guess you could just say "tough luck, David".

My mother loved children but she had a mean streak. When they first got me she would threaten to send me back to the orphanage. One time she actually had someone stop outside the house with their car and pretend they were going to take me back to the orphanage. I remember being sent up to my bedroom to put on my shoes. It must have taken me 20 minutes to tie my shoes, while I was crying. When they first got me she constantly threatened to send me back to the orphanage, when I misbehaved. Another time when she was giving me a bath in the kitchen sink, she hurt my penis by scrubbing it so hard with a washcloth. I had not been circumcised, so the tip of the penis was very tender. I told her it hurt, but she kept right on. Periodically a lady from Catholic Services would stop to check on how things were going with my new family. I was threatened before she got there not to say anything bad or she would take me back to the orphanage. As you know a young child wants to do what his parents asked and I didn't want to go back to the orphanage, so I would lie.

After the orphanage threat didn't work anymore, she threatened to send me to St. Charles, Illinois. Apparently there was a reform school there where uncontrollable children were sent. Quite often I would get beatings from her for bad performance on my report card. Almost every time I brought my report card home from school, I would get ostracized and spanked with whatever was handy, usually a yardstick. That is back in the day when they were quarter-inch thick. It wasn't the grades so much as the comments on behavior. When they first got me I used to wet the bed and I would get a spanking for that. No more water after six o'clock. Later we found out it was a nervous condition brought on by the trauma of leaving the orphanage.

I didn't always understand the actions of my parents. When starting first-grade I was told to stay with Kyle. When it was time to come home from school, Kyle went with some other children a different way home. I knew that wasn't right, so I went the same way mother brought us to school. Walking back home everything looked different. I thought I was lost. When I got to School Street, I stopped at this lady's house and asked her to call my mother. Mother came to pick me up shortly after that. When I got in the car she gave me hell for not staying with Kyle. When we got home Kyle wasn't there yet and everybody was worried. I was sent up to my room, after a licking without supper. Kyle arrived many hours later with hugs and kisses greeting him. It seemed to me that I did the right thing, but caught hell for it. It is really difficult to understand the rationale with this type of behavior by my parents.

There were some good things that happened during my early years. I remember my dad taking me to the shop Christmas party and receiving a gift. We also went on picnics and played softball. My mother used to take me shopping with her and we would stop at the Woolworth Dime Store for lunch. She also allowed me to walk around the store on my own. Whenever she would take the car to get serviced, I got to stay in the car while it was being raised up on a hoist. Mother would always let me play outside with Kyle until dark, which was always fun. My dad took me to the motorcycle races at the Pecatonica County fair.

Years later when we were on the farm, Kyle and I took a tricycle and tied it behind my horse and pretended it was a motorcycle. This worked until the horse got mad. She took off like a shot out of a gun and left the tricycle and me in the dust.

Quite often I would have to stay home with my Aunt Diane while my parents went golfing with the neighbors. My aunt was my mentor. She was always good to me. However, she didn't mind telling my parents, if I had been a bad boy. Here comes another spanking. Life wasn't easy for me. I grew up tough. I guess God knows when people should have children. This couple had no idea how to raise a child.

CHAPTER 3

THE FARM

When I was eight years old my folks decided to move to the farm. I found out many years later, it was because of my mother. As I stated earlier my mother was a very jealous person. My dad was a good-looking man and the women gave him a great deal of attention. This bothered my mother, so she felt that she had to get my dad away from the city. She thought moving to a farm would be the solution. Neither of them knew anything about farming. One of the things they soon learned was to milk the cows on time. Especially when they had company. When they first went on the farm, they would milk after the company left. They would not get done milking until late at night. The cows were milked by hand. Later we got a milking machine. Fortunately I was too young to milk by hand.

I remember when my folks decided to buy the farm. They traded their house in town including several war bonds they cashed in. I was in awe of all the bonds they had. There were enough war bonds to fill my dad's lunch box. Dad bought everything, including livestock and machinery.

My dad began farming with a Farmall F-20 tractor and a team of horses. Dad buying the farm as is, was a mistake. The equipment used was horse drawn and would break down often. Most of the equipment being horse drawn required a slow speed and wide turns. Because we used a tractor, breakdowns happened quite often. Usually when going too fast or making too short of turns.

When dad first tried to plant corn with a horse drawn corn planter, he didn't understand why he was dropping twelve kernels at a time, when there should only be one to three. He had a friend from Rockford come down to the farm and figure out the problem. It turned out he had put in the wrong planter plates. The plates in the planter were for soybeans instead of corn.

We did not use the horses that much, so we shortened the tongues on most of the horse-drawn equipment. This didn't stop dad from the equipment break downs because he went too fast. One time Dad had me ride on the dump rake to pick up the loose hay that was missed by the baler. He went so fast the rake would trip on it's own. He would look back at me and ask, "What the hell did you do that for? You damn dummy". I tried to explain that when the wheels went over a rock, the cog on the wheel would go into the spline gear and trip the rake. It didn't do any good, he went like hell in sixth gear practically throwing me off the seat. There were a number of episodes like this.

Another time I remember we had to load some loose hay in a lower field. It had rained and the drain field had ruptured creating a large muddy area. I said, we better not try to go through it. He decided to put the tractor in sixth gear and try it anyway. Guess what, we got stuck. The tractor sank about a foot. No matter how we tried, we just went in deeper. I ran over to our neighbors and asked if he could use his Farmall "M" tractor. He came over and saw our plight and said he didn't dare try and pull us out. He was afraid he would also be stuck in the mud. The next day I came up with the brilliant idea of using a wooden post and a log chain and securing the post to the tires. When I put the tractor in gear and slowly tried to back up, the tractor would raise up when the post hit the ground. It was like trying to get a wounded elephant out of the mud, but it worked. I got the tractor out of the mud and drove around the soft area. I ended up loading the hay by hand.

As I stated earlier my dad always needed someone to be with him. This led to some problems with my mother. For example, when it came time for threshing or silo filling, all the farmers in the area got together and went from one farm to another. Because our farm was small, it didn't take long for our threshing or silo filling. Dad had to be gone several days on the other farms and this didn't set well with my mother. Consequently, they would get into a verbal fight. Eventually my dad had enough of the farm. He said "I can make money a damn sight easier in a factory". Dad decided to go back to Ingersoll's. Unfortunately he had to begin all over again, earning his vacations and starting at a lower salary than when he left. He was back with all his working buddies and that meant a lot to him. Several of the guys from Ingesoll's would come down to the farm and hunt rabbits and pheasants with him.

My dad really wanted to move back to town. He hated the farm in many ways. My mother said, "We can't take David to the city. He will just get into trouble". I became the pawn whenever dad wanted to go back to town. I believe this to be one of the reasons why my dad disliked me. He felt I was the reason he had to stay on the farm.

I enjoyed threshing because I got to drive all of the different tractors on the various farms. After the threshing season, the farmers got together and gave me $20. I remember going home and crying, because I had never received anything like this before. I wasn't expecting anything. I just enjoyed driving all of the different tractors and receiving accolades from the farmers.

We had 35 acres of woods that we used for pasture. The woods weren't really any good for pasture. In order to make up for the poor grass, I had to herd the cows along the roadside every day during the summer. I also had to tie the small calves and horse to fence posts along the roadside. This usually meant carrying water a great distance morning, noon and night. Generally I moved them once each day. I remember my dad telling me, "Be sure and give them plenty of water. It's the cheapest thing we got". He of course didn't have to carry the water. Each calf took about 5 gallons each watering.

My dad going back to work, meant leaving at 6am and getting home approximately 6pm. Because of this, I had to help my mother with the chores. Even before this, I always had to be with him and help clean the barn and do the milking. One evening my dad came home drunk and couldn't navigate the next morning. He had a blinding headache (he would get headaches quite often) so he laid down on some straw and went to sleep. I knew how to operate the DelaValve milking machine, so I milked the cows myself, thinking I would get a pat on the back. I always wanted to show my parents that I could do things (my mistake). After Dad discovered I could milk on my own, milking became one of my permanent chores. I milked the cows morning and night. This was the beginning of my taking over all the chores.

I had to get up at 5am each morning to milk, clean the barn, feed the cows, sheep and hogs. To feed the cows silage, I had to climb up about twenty feet into the silo to throw down the silage. In the winter this became a difficult task, because the silage would freeze to the sides of the steel silo. Generally it froze in about a foot and a half from the edge. It required a lot of effort to break it loose with the silage fork. In addition my dad never had a roof over the silo, so I always had snow to contend with too. The next thing was to let the cows out for water, because our barn was not equipped with drinking cups at each stanchion. During this time I would scatter the silage in the manger. Next climb up in the haymow and throw down enough hay for twenty cows and place it in the manger. The cows knew the feed would be there when they came in from drinking water. This made it easy to get them back in the barn. For those of you who are not familiar with farms, all of the cows had their own stanchions. I was always impressed how each cow knew her stanchion. The hogs were next and they were fed ear corn (corn on the cob to you) and slop. Slop is a mixture of oat, mineral and yeast. The sheep were fed hay and given water. The water had to be carried by hand, bucket by bucket to the hogs and sheep. The water was poured into their respective watering trough. On weekends, I cleaned the calf pens, chicken coup and ground feed. The corn was fun to grind, but the oats took forever. I was only in seventh grade at the time I began doing all this by myself. The school bus came at seven o'clock. All the chores had to be done by then, including the milking, before the milk truck came. The milk had to be put into milk cans and placed in the milk house water cooling tank. The milk was picked up each morning every day of the week.

I need to give my mother credit here. The chickens were hers, so she fed and watered them as well as collect the eggs. I had the dirty work of cleaning those damn roosts and floor full of rat holes. They had been covered over with lids from tin cans. The forks and shovels would always catch on the corners of these. The manure on the roosts would get packed so hard you had to use a scraper to break it loose.

Cleaning the barn took quite a while. We did not have a barn cleaner. In fact nothing was mechanized. I removed the manure from the gutter, one fork at a time and walked to the end of the barn to throw it on a pile. The calf pens were cleaned the same way on weekends. When cleaning the calf pens, the manure went directly into a spreader and taken out to the field. In the spring, I would load the manure pile and spread it on the field. Heaven forbid, should the drag chain break on the spreader. When the chain breaks you have to unload the spreader by hand then fix the chain.

When spring came, it was time to do field work, such as disk and plow the fields. My dad would try to do this after work. This didn't give him much time before dark. I decided one night after chores, that I would try my hand at plowing. After making one trip around the field my mother tried to stop me by standing in front of the tractor. She said, "You aren't plowing right". I told her, "I know how to plow. Get out of my way". I put the tractor in gear, let out the clutch and started forward. She got out of the way and said, "I'm going to tell your dad". Well! Dad must have been satisfied with the plowing because I never heard a word from him. From that time on I did all of the fieldwork. Sometimes I would try to plow after the evening milking. I always appreciated it, when mother would do the milking for me so I could get more plowing done.

Back in the 50s and early 60s, to prepare a field for planting required plowing, disking and dragging. Today farmers do what is called no—till. This is accomplished by using a spring tooth harrow or a chisel plow. Farmers also use herbicides to keep the weeds down. The use of herbicides requires less tilling of the soil.

In the spring and summer when it came time for haying, we put up the hay loose. We would hitch a hay loader behind a hayrack, then use a team of horses to pull the rack. After the first year, I loaded hay by myself. This was the easy part. After I got the hay from the field to the barn, I had to pull it up into the barn. The tractor and/or horses were hitched to a rope on the backside of the barn. A hayfork was attached to the front side of the rope. Before I could unload the hay wagon, I had to get either my mother or sister to drive the tractor or command the horses. I put stakes in the ground, so they knew just how far to go with each successive pull. After the hay was in the mow, I had to go up into loft and mow the hay. Mowing is using a three—tine pitchfork and moving the hay from where it was dropped, to the outer walls in order to make room for the next load.

Later on when balers were available we hired someone to bale the hay. Hay balers were not available, when we first started farming. Eventually, we also hired someone to plant our corn.

Before the farmer started baling, I would get wagons the day before, from several farmers and have them available for pulling behind the baler. By doing this, I didn't have to pick the bales up off the ground. One year I had over 3000 bales to pick up. Haying by myself was not an easy task. Each bale had to be picked up and placed on the hayrack. After I had several bales on the rack, I would climb up on the rack and stack them. I could put as many as 68 bales on a rack. Once I had a full load, I took them up to the barn for unloading. This was accomplished by the use of a large grapple hook, which held six bales at a time. The procedure for getting the bales in the barn was the same as when I put up loose hay. I usually handled each bale three times. Needless to say haying was my most hated job. The only job comparable to this was putting in fences.

Before we could put bales in the barn, the floor had to be reinforced. We did this by using heavy 10 by 12 timbers for support.

One time I asked my dad to help me stack the excess hay outside. I had more hay than the barn could hold, so it had to be stack outside. I got up on the hayrack and started handing bales down. As he began to stack the bales, he wasn't inner locking them. "You're doing it wrong", I said. That was a mistake. I tried to show him, but he just jumped off the stack and said, "Stack the God damn hay yourself." He went into the house. That was the last I saw of him.

Most of the things I learned about raising cattle and doing fieldwork were from other farmers. Later I learned from taking Agriculture in school. My parents allowed me to have my own livestock. I had one cow (raised from twins), one sow with a litter of six and twelve sheep for my Ag projects. This was supposed to be the pay for my work. I think they got one hell of a deal! Of course my room and board was included.

While I had the Chester White sow, she never had more than a litter of six pigs. My mother felt bad for me, so she took the sow and gave me a different one. This same sow had a litter of twelve the next year. The pig I traded for had seven, so goes my luck again. One of the goals in FFA (Future Farmers of America) was to have a ton litter. This meant the total weight of all the pigs in a litter equal 2000 pounds when fully grown. It's impossible to make a ton litter with seven. One hundred ninety to two hundred twenty pounds were considered the finishing weight for breeding or butchering. You can see I was nowhere near one ton.

One of the worst accidents I had on the farm was losing part of my small finger on my right hand. I was getting a bucket of water for the house. It was raining and the belt was slipping on the pulley of the Pump Jack. I tried to help the belt by turning the pulley with my hands. In the process I caught my little finger between the belt and the pulley. I tried to work my hand through, but it started hurting so much I hollered for someone to shut the pump off. This was a very painful experience. My mother took me to the doctor in Byron. He took one look at my finger, grabbed a pair of scissors and cut it the rest of the way off. He then gave me a shot for pain. Then we drove to Rockford for surgery. I had a few other accidents over my farming years, such as smashing my hand between the running gear and a wagon box. My fingers, after I got my hand free, were about a half-inch thick. I was trying to remove the wagon from the running gear, so it could be used on a different wagon. The wagon was three quarters full of ground oats. I was fortunate I never got caught in the corn picker. Whenever the corn picker would plug up, I would try to clear the jam by pulling out the debris from the husking rollers, without stopping the machine. Many farm accidents were caused from corn pickers.

Speaking of corn picking, this wasn't an easy task either. It was right up there with haying. My dad had bought a picker where the shute came out the side. All I had was a hayrack that was 8 feet wide and 16 feet long. (I made this rack in Ag.) Because of the eight foot width, it required stopping the picker after the wagon was partially loaded. Then get into the wagon and shovel the corn towards the back, then the front as it filled. As the wagon filled I had to make several stops to even out the load.

I had torn the old corncrib down one summer. The crib was in terrible shape. The floors were full of rat holes and the sides were leaning. When dad saw that I had torn down the old crib, he let loose with some expletives. He said, "The old corncrib was good enough". "Ah, that's good enough" would be his response for many of the things we did on the farm.

Dad and I put up a new wire crib. Instead of pouring a nice cement floor, dad decided to use some of the broken up concrete from the hog feeding floor. This made a rather cobbled up floor. However, this was better than the rat hole floor we had in the old wooden crib. We didn't have an elevator for the crib, so I had to shovel all of corn in by hand. This wasn't easy because I had to throw the corn over the top of the crib. I threw the corn through the opening that was meant for an elevator. My dad's penny pinching always made it seem like we had to do every thing the hard way.

Another example of doing things the hard way, whenever I had to build another fence, I had to tear down an old one and try to reuse the wire. Most of our fences were old and rusty and grown up with brush. I would have to clean out the fence row, before I could remove the wire and posts. Much of the wire would break when I tried to roll it up. The rusty breaking wire made fencing very difficult. Pulling out the old rusty staples from the posts was next to impossible. Whenever I had to build something out of wood, I had to use the wood and nails from the patterns we tore apart. We never used new wood or nails. Even dad's handsaws were rusty, with little or no set. Thus to build something was a "bitch".

Another difficult thing was clearing seven acres of woods for my class project. Rather than have the man use the bulldozer to clear the land, he just had him forced over the trees. My dad and I dragged all the trees off with a tractor and chain. He drove the tractor, while I hooked and unhooked the chain. I planned to plant corn on this land for my agriculture project, once it was cleared.

One time, we tried to mount an off brand manure loader onto the tractor. Part of the mounting required lifting the heavy hydraulic cylinders. My dad tried to hold them up, while I put the bolt through the mounting holes. If I didn't get the bolt through right away, he would let go with expletives. I discovered I could put the loader on myself, by just raising one end of the cylinder at a time and fastened it to the tractor.

Whenever my dad needed a tool or wrench, he would always send me looking for it. He never put anything back, so I would have to go from building to building trying find whatever it was he needed. One time we were down in the field and something broke. He needed a wrench to fix whatever it was. I started towards the barn, but apparently I wasn't moving fast enough. He started picking up clods of dirt and throwing them at me. Once again, He let go with a few expletives to hurry up. He was a man of little or no patience and a quick temper. One time he came after me with a pitch fork because he didn't think I was moving fast enough.

One time I remember most vividly is when my dad and I got into an argument and he chased me off the farm with a pitchfork. As I started to go he told me to take off my boots because they belong to him. Back then the roads were all gravel and made my feet sore. After I walked about a mile my mother came along in the car and tried to get me to come back. After talking for several minutes and begging me to come back, I decided to get in the car. I don't think my dad thought about the consequences of me leaving. Me leaving meant he would have to do all the chores along with mother. He would also have to take over all the other work I was doing.

You might say life on the farm was no picnic. I don't recall of ever being asked to do something. It seems as though I was always told or commanded to do something. It used to irritate me when my mother would tell me to do things on the weekend. I had already planned to do such things as grind feed, or clean her chicken coop. My folks were always on my case for something or other. I became very paranoid, I would think I could hear them calling out "David" even though they weren't. This caused me to be very timid in class at school. I would practically break into a sweat, when asked a question by the teacher for fear of giving the wrong answer. I didn't want to appear dumb by the other students. I think this came from being beaten down and demoralized by my parents all the time. I never seem to do anything right or get credit for a job well done. It behooves me, why I cried when my parents said they were selling the farm.

One of my prized accomplishments was in 1955, when I won the State Soil and Conservation Award. This would not have happened without the help of the County agent, my Agriculture teacher and the Agriculture teacher from Byron, Illinois.

This all came about when the Ag. Teacher from Byron was putting anhydrous ammonia (nitrogen) on my cornfield. He had seen that I had cleared the seven acres of woods for my corn project. In addition, with the help of the County agent, I put our farm into strip cropping. The County agent drove his truck through the fields. I followed him with a tractor and plow. Before we could do this however, I had to tear out all the line fence rows separating the fields. My Ag. teacher help me layout and build waterways using a plow and tractor. The large water way was completed using a bulldozer.

My teacher took several pictures and placed them in a book. This book was the only thing that was used in competition for the district and regional contest. To win the state I had to take my book down to Champaign Urbana and meet with a committee of Ag. Teachers. I didn't think I had a chance of winning. My book looked pretty skimpy, when I saw the other contestants' books. After the Ag teachers had met with all the contestants, they called me back into the room and told me I had won. They said that there wasn't any question that I did the work. Often times the dads did the work and the son took the credit. My parents and I drove to Champaign Urbana to receive my award. I flew in an airplane back from Urbana. My folks stayed there to visit with friends.

Another accomplishment I was proud of was being chosen by the American Legion to participate in Premier Boys State Conference at the University of Illinois. We participated in government activities, including military maneuvers and leadership. Upon returning home I gave an oral report to the local Chapter. I was selected because I was an outstanding student in farming and the community.

I recognize that working on the farm was hard, but it also taught me responsibility. I was known by several of the farmers, including the Ogle County agent. They all were aware of my abilities and hard work and that I operated the farm. I had several offers to manage other farms, when I graduated from high school. One of the offers I received was from the Mayor of Stillman Valley. He owned the local grain elevator and a large farm. He said, "If you come and work for me, I will build you anything you want and help you purchase equipment." Even the County agent asked me to come and work for him. I had always wanted to attend college, so I turned down their offers. I was the first one in the family to attend college. In fact, I was one of the first students to go to college from Stillman Valley High School. I don't know to this day, why my Ag. teacher told me not to mention my winning the Soil and Water Management Award to other students. I never had a chance to celebrate my winning or get any publicity in the local paper. This just seemed to be the way my life went.

Being in agriculture gave me a chance to do some neat things. I remember showing my sheep and cow at the Stephenson County Fair. I, along with other classmates, won several awards. I never did get a first with my animals.

In order to haul the calves and sheep to the fair, I had to build a rack for the back of the truck. Guess what lumber I used. Being at the fair with my friends was a lot of fun. We played several games on the midway. We tried for a radio by tossing rings over bottles. Together we spent $21 to win a radio. We probably could have bought the same thing for eight dollars.

Before the animals were shown, they had to be groomed. The grooming was done inside a large barn. For the cows they had a cemented area for washing and grooming them. We slept with the animals and talked about girls. As I remember we won several ribbons, but very few blue ribbons. Besides showing the animals, I had a lot of fun. This was my first time away from the farm. Once again my mother came through and did the chores.

When living on a farm you don't have the time to play with other kids, like those in town. You are alone most of the time because of all the work that has to be done. Whenever I felt sorry for myself, I would go and pet my horse. She was the only one on the farm that showed me any affection. I would place my arms around her neck and she would press her chin against my back.

She was a very smart horse. She had figured out how to open the barn door. I was continually being blamed for not locking the door. I had stacked baled hay in the calf pens that weren't being used. Invariably she and the cows would be in the barn eating the hay. Jill also discovered how to undo the chain around the main gate and let all the cattle out.

Jill was a spoiled horse. She never liked saddles, so I would ride her bareback most of the time. In order to catch her for riding, I would hide the bridle in my shirt and hold out an ear of corn. She always seemed to know when I had the bridle with me. She ran with the cows most of the time. The only time she was separated from the cows is when I kept her in the barnyard at night, so she could take me to the cows in the woods.

Jill never liked it when I would hook her up to the buggy. Whenever she passed our driveway, she would fight to turn in. Another thing she did not like was a puddle of water. She could stop on a dime, throw you off and try to go around the water. The interesting thing about Jill is when I would fall off, she would stand there until I got back on her.

When I went to college, we had to sell the farm. Jill was the hardest thing to see go. My parents could not run the farm on their own. Selling the farm was their only option.

Prior to the day of the auction, I spent that day and night working on the tractor. I couldn't get it running, so I called the John Deere dealer in Rockford and they got it running for the sale. That was a close call, the tractor goes down in value if the farmers can't see it running. I also lined up all the equipment in rows and made sure everything was in working order.

I remember crying later the day of the sale. I had poured my heart and soul into the farm. I had doubled the value of the farm by all the things I had done. I built a new, three fourths of a mile, line fence, painted all the buildings, including the house and barn. Something funny happened when I was painting the barn. I had just climbed the ladder to the peak of the barn and got ready to start spraying. All of a sudden the ladder started to slide down the barn. I stayed with it until I came all the way down the side of the barn. You could see two parallel marks coming down the barn. It so happened the barnyard was muddy, therefore the legs of the ladder were not on solid ground. I had also put in waterways and change the land to strip crop farming to avoid soil erosion. Our land was quite hilly so soil runoff was a problem.

CHAPTER 4

MY COUSIN JOINS US
ON THE FARM

In the fall of 1954 my cousin Kyle came to live with us. His parents were having difficulties making ends meet. His dad worked for J. I Case in Rockford, Illinois and it seemed like they were always on strike. My mother suggested Kyle come and stay on the farm with us. My mother talked it over with her sister and they decided it would be good for them and Kyle. Kyle came to live with us for the next two years. Having him with us gave me a little more freedom. I also had someone my age. I could converse and do things with him. Kyle being six months older, he had a driver's license and could drive us to school. Before I was able to get a driver's license, I had to be 16. Illinois had just changed the driving age from 15 to 16, before a teenager could get a license. Wouldn't you know, they changed it in July and my birthday was in September, just my luck.

Having Kyle on the farm made some of the chores easier for me. Having two people doing the work together was a blessing. When Kyle first came to the farm, it took him a while to get adjusted. He came from a school of 1200 students. Stillman Valley only had 150 students. Coming from a large city he was more up to date in the way city kids wore their clothes. For example, his jeans rested below the hips. Most of us came from a small town and were not up to the latest styles. We wore our jeans above the waist and kept our shirts tucked in. Most of the kids accepted Kyle right away. He became involved in many of the activities at school, especially sports.

Kyle joined the football team with me and was the field goal kicker and a backup quarterback. He was also active in track and field. Kyle chose to participate in the high jump and pole vaulting. I on the other hand was a miler and ran in the 440 relay race. When practicing for the mile I would run on the railroad tracks, which ran right by our farm. The distance from our farm to school was about 2 miles. Once at school I took a shower and got ready for classes. Kyle and I both participated in several track meets. In football I played several positions. I usually played where they needed strength and/or speed. Most of the time I played on the offense and defensive end. We played six—man football. In six—man football we had to go 15 yards for a first down instead of the normal 10 yards, most people are familiar with an eleven men team. Because our team was so exceptional, all six seniors, we were made team captains. We won the "Route 72" conference in both our junior and senior years.

I was also involved in the class play for two years. I helped the class raise money all four years. Our senior year the class chose to see the sights of New York. The trip to New York took us eighteen hours by train. When we arrived in New York, we all had food poisoning. One of our classmates became so ill, she ended up in the hospital. While we were in New York we had an opportunity to go on to Washington DC, but we chose not to. Now that I'm older, I regret that we didn't take that opportunity.

Kyle enrolled in agriculture classes with me and joined the FFA. My mother gave him a calf and a pig for his project. He was more fortunate than I when the pigs farrowed. My sow had a litter of six again and his had seven. After that year my mother traded pigs with him. Would you believe the same sow had 12 piglets that year. This was important to us because we always wanted a ton litter. In order to have a ton litter, the sow must farrow eight or more baby pigs to achieve that.

Kyle not having lived on a farm before was in awe of the many things that happened. Seeing calves and pigs born along with some of the animals dying from time to time was unsettling.

One of our responsibilities in Agriculture class was to keep track of all of the feed given to our project animals. In class we put this information in a project book. Some of the information in the project book included: calculation on weight gain, the cost and amount of feed being given to each animal. If we had a cow milking, we also had to weigh and test the milk for butterfat content. We had Guernsey cows that always tested high. Their butterfat test always ran about 5.0. A typical Holstein would test around 3.7.

In May we began to do field work. We only had one tractor. This didn't make sense now that I had another person available. I decided to go over to the equipment dealer in

Byron and see what I could buy with the money I had earned from setting pins at the bowling alley. The dealer let me buy a 1937 John Deere "B" for $300. I still owed $80, but he knew I was good for it. Only being 15 years old, I wasn't sure he would let me take it. But as I said earlier, I was well known in the County for all of my activities and achievements. When I got home with the tractor my mother asked me whom the tractor belong to. I told her I bought the tractor from the John Deere dealer in Byron. I didn't tell mother I still owed $80 on it. She discovered the balance owed when the bill came. I was surprised my mother didn't get on my case after seeing there was a balance due. Mother fortunately could see the advantage in having a second tractor.

It was nice having another person help me with the fieldwork. I did all the cultivating and mowing of the hay. We had a little contest to see who could get the darkest tan. By fall it looked as though, we were from another culture.

Kyle was somewhat of a "prima donna". He only did things he wanted to do. He did however take care of his own project. He never helped with the plowing or mowing of the hay. He didn't mind disking or dragging the fields, after I plowed them in preparation for planting.

Besides working on the farm, we also had our fun. One of the things we used to do, was grab the tails of the calves in the pasture and see who could hang on the longest. Sometimes we would get on the backs of the calves and ride them. We would pretend we were riding bucking Broncos in a rodeo.

At first we would go out with my buddies together. Later on Kyle became interested in a girl over in Byron. Once a girl was involved, we went our separate ways. I had been going out with my buddies since my freshman year. Several of my classmates were a year older than I and most of them were allowed to drive their dads' cars.

My mother, depending on her mood, would let Kyle take the family car to see his girlfriend. Most of the time my buddies and I would go to a movie or just ride around. Sometimes we would stop for a pizza or go to this restaurant in Byron and get a sweet roll. The sweet roll was warmed on a grill and heavily buttered, "Man, were they good". Along with the sweet rolls, we also had a cup of coffee and played the jukebox.

I usually traveled with two or three other guys. One person in particular was very good at driving. He could've been in the Daytona 500. I remember one night, we were driving down "Route 2" going 90 miles an hour in a rainstorm. The rain was coming down so hard you could only see about 10 feet in front of the hood. I'll have to admit this was a white-knuckle ride. There were times we took curves on two wheels. I swear you could touch the pavement.

We used to race our cars on "Route 72" between Byron and Stillman Valley. It was lucky we never met oncoming cars. We did some dangerous things, as all teenagers do. I know going at that speed, I ruined the engine in my dad's Rambler station wagon. It wasn't built to go at that speed.

I remember one time, Kyle took the neighbor's daughter out on a date. After they had gone to a movie, he decided to park in her dad's field near the mouth of Stillman Creek. When he started to go back to her place, the car got stuck. He had to walk about a mile up to her dad's place to have him get his tractor and pull him out. Her dad wondered why they were down in the field so far off the road. I think Kyle became paranoid about her dad. He felt every time he was in the same room as her dad, he felt him staring at him.

One time Kyle wanted to see his girlfriend in Byron. He met her at a football game. My mother said he couldn't use the car to go and see her. So Kyle walked about 3 miles to see this girl. He could be quite stubborn at times. He didn't always want to do the same things I wanted to do. There were times he didn't want to go somewhere and we both stayed home. I was somewhat hamstrung because I couldn't drive yet.

One time he was eating breakfast and disagreed with something my mother said. Mother was frying eggs on the stove. She turned around and hit him on the head with the spatula. He was so surprised. He jumped up from his chair with his fist doubled, as though he was going to hit her. Nothing happened but he told her, "Don't ever to do that again". Generally we all got along quite well. I did however tolerate many of his changing moods.

I never had a steady girl in the high school. I was always afraid I would get emotionally attached. I felt I needed my freedom. Generally I never went with a girl more than three times. Anymore than this and they think they own you. Also I was afraid of getting hurt. I had enough of being emotionally hurt from my parents. Therefore I was always on guard.

I wish I could remember all of the things we did on the farm and in school. Kyle has a much better memory about all our experiences together. One time in later years, my wife and family went out to the state of Oregon to visit him and his family. As we visited he began reminiscing about the days on the farm. His daughter would say, "Here comes story number 49". Kyle loved the farm. He discussed his farm life with his children often. Even today when I talk to Kyle on the phone, he always brings up the farm. Being on the farm was a major event in his life and I'm glad I could be part of it.

Kyle and I graduated from Stillman Valley together. We both decided to go to college at Platteville, Wisconsin together. He chose to go to Platteville with me and play football. He was good enough to go with the traveling team, but he never had an opportunity to start.

CHAPTER 5

COLLEGE YEARS

B efore my mother would let me go to college, she said I had to improve my reading skills. So she enrolled me in a remedial reading class at Rockford College. My instructor later became the Superintendent for Rockford Public Schools. After taking the course I improved my reading speed from 40 words per minute to 82 words per minute and increased my comprehension. One of the things I wished they taught in high school was how to take class notes. In college I tried to take down everything the instructor said and that was a disaster. I even used the tape recorder in some of my classes. Reviewing the tape recorder required too much of my time, so that really didn't work.

In the fall of 1956 I started college in Industrial Arts. The first thing the new freshman had to take was entrance exams. I scored high enough, so I didn't have to take the 101 courses in English or math. Some of the Industrial Arts courses were challenging for me. Most of the other students had Industrial Arts classes in middle school and high school. They didn't teach Industrial Arts classes in

Stillman Valley. Drafting and woodworking were the most difficult and time-consuming subjects. I was "all thumbs", when I first began the drafting courses. In woodworking I wasn't familiar with all the different machines, so I was kind of behind the eight ball. By my sophomore year, I had caught up to everyone. Sometimes the general requirements could be the most difficult. Psychology was a foreign language to me and history wasn't any better. I only got one "F" in college and that was in math analysis. The reason for the "F" was I had quit the course after the six weeks deadline. My physics and biology courses along with all of my Industrial Arts courses were all I could handle. My math professor wouldn't let me drop the class, so I took an automatic "F". The Industrial Arts courses were all two credits. Because of this you usually had to take four or five classes. Each of these classes required one hour of lecture and two labs, two hours each week. A class that drove me nuts was library science. Filling out those damn catalog cards was ridiculous. From memory on a test, we had to make out an author card, subject card and a title card. Today everything is done when you order a book from the publisher for the library. The cards come with the book, so they can be uploaded into a computer retrieval system.

Most libraries put everything in a data retrieval system. The day of the card catalog in college libraries is over.

Biology was a scary subject at first because the instructor stated, "One half of you will fail this course". In order not to fail the course I would go over my notes every night. I also studied the previous days class notes. I continued to do this all through the course. It paid off because I got an "A" in biology. A course I thoroughly enjoyed was physics. I flunked my first weekly exam. Formerly, the course had previous been taught by another instructor, who automatically gave the Industrial Arts students a "C". The new instructor said we would get whatever we earn for a grade. What made the course difficult was the Industrial Arts students were enrolled in second semester without having the first semester. The first semester physics was where the mechanics were taught. The thing that helped me the most was the skill of the professor. In addition I would study and work through all the problems during the week then teach some of my classmates the problems before the Friday exam. You always learn material much better when you teach someone else. I ended up getting an "A" for the course.

My major was Industrial Arts and my minor was Social Sciences and Mathematics. When I did my student teaching I had no difficulty with Industrial Arts. It was a different story teaching Social Studies. I had to teach European History, which wasn't my long suit. In fact I was going to quit teaching Social Studies. I went to the Dean of Education and asked him if I could try another teaching assignment. Dr. Hutchison convinced me to stay with it. I did stay the rest of the semester teaching Social Studies and got a "B".

Some of my other courses were a joke. For example, at Christmas break the Economics instructor gave all the girls the regurgitated pelts from his owl Klacker. Their assignment was to take the pelts home and label all parts of a mouse. I never did understand why the girls got the pelts and the boys didn't. But surprisingly enough the girls came back with the parts of the mouse labeled.

A course I was totally petrified in was the required Speech course. I was always nervous when I had to stand up in front of my peers. I can remember the first time I got up to speak, I broke into a sweat and my knees became rubbery. I made it through the course with a "C". My Speech professor was an absolute nut. This dude was off the wall.

He would have all the girls sit in the front row, so he could see up their dresses. Also he would grab the rope from the blinds and walk across the front of the room. When he got to the other side, he would let go and the rope would bang against the other wall. One year later, he was let go from the University for being with a student in his room, doing whatever gays do.

Every year for the Homecoming parade the Industrial Arts school would enter a float. Because they always placed first, we decided to just enter a complementary float and give someone else a chance to win first place.

Another facet of college was dorm life. My cousin and I roomed together our freshman year. Several times Kyle would go out at night and come back with the dry heaves from drinking too much. He also played poker with the veterans from the Mining School. Most of the time he would lose all the money he had. One thing that wasn't tolerated at the University in those days was a student coming back to the dorm drunk. He never got caught, but I saw others get thrown out of school for the same reason. Eventually Kyle's gambling caused him to have to quit school. Kyle was able to finish his sophomore year. After that year he decided to go to Naval Air Force where he served for four years.

I never understood why my mother and my Aunt Diane always sent him money and never me. I guess they felt sorry for Kyle because he came from a poor family. For some reason my mother thought I had plenty of money. My sophomore year, I waited on tables for my meals and room. On Friday evenings after closing, I would scrub the floors and clean the French fryer.

One of the students in the dorm must have weighed 450 pounds. Fred controlled the television in the dorm. One time Kyle and I got into his pants together. He saw us and started to chase us down the hall. Man that guy could move! He never did catch us or we would have been dead. No one would give Fred a ride to school in their vehicles, because he would break down the seat due to his weight.

College wasn't much fun for me, because of the lack of money and time. All of my courses in Industrial Arts required lots of outside time and work. The lack of money limited what I could do for activities. I lived on a cup of coffee for breakfast and chili for supper in my sophomore and junior year. Needless to say, I lost a lot of weight while in my first three years of college.

My last year of college, I married my lovely wife Darlene. She helped me survive my Senior year by waitressing at Mel's Diner.

It also helped when her parents brought us eggs. Darlene also did my typing because I could not type.

My senior year courses were quite easy. I had taken all of my requirements before then. I knew I would have student teaching, so I wanted to have all my requirements out of the way.

I graduated in 1960 with a Bachelor of Science Degree from Wisconsin State College and Institute of Technology. It is now called the University of Wisconsin—Platteville.

After my wife and I were married, we found an upstairs apartment near the college. Darlene's sister stayed with us that year. She was an entering freshman with an Education Major.

When we were placing our clothes in the dresser drawers, we noticed these bugs. Darlene or I didn't have a clue as to what these bugs were. We discovered some time later they were cockroaches.

Later during my senior year, Darlene changed jobs (for a little more money and better tips) and worked as a waitress at Ed's Truck Stop. I worked there evenings for a while, but it was just too much along with my schoolwork and student teaching. It did not give me enough time to sleep. Darlene also did all my typing and architectural sketches. I could do detail drawings, but I have no artistic abilities. Unfortunately I can't type either.

CHAPTER 6

TEACHING AND WORKING

A concern when you're about to graduate is getting a teaching position. My first opportunity to teach was in Boulder, Colorado. I didn't take that teaching position because it required my flying out to Colorado for an interview. I couldn't afford the cost of flying out there. Today many of the superintendents will pay for your travel. My first opportunity to interview was with Mr. Neus from Plainfield, Illinois. He drove to Platteville to recruit a new teacher for a new position. After my interview with him, he hired me on the spot. It so happened, he wanted someone to teach some Agriculture classes along with several Industrial Arts classes. The current Agriculture teacher was not performing in the classroom. It turned out the only way they could get rid of the former Agriculture teacher was to eliminate Agriculture. This was an Agriculture community, so he wondered if I could teach some things in Agriculture. I developed a course called Home and Farm Construction. This course seemed to satisfy all the farmers' children. We repaired motors, sharpen disks, repaired tractors and did welding on farm equipment.

The shop didn't have some of the equipment I needed for electronics, electricity and metals. Fortunately the school board was willing to let me buy lumber for building the necessary mechanics tables and order several pieces of equipment. They also allowed me to buy several pieces of electronic test equipment. My electronic students constructed all of the electronic test equipment in class under my supervision.

I taught in Plainfield for one year. I also coached football in addition to working for Bryant Aluminum designing steel buildings, in order to make enough money. Our first child was born that year and put a strain on our budget. I was only making $4500 along with coaching.

When I left Plainfield I received a very complementary letter signed by all of the members of the Plainfield School Board thanking me for all the things I had done for the school.

My second year of teaching I wanted to get into a larger system. I thought by getting into the larger system, they would have all the machine tools and equipment. I was able to secure a teaching position at Roosevelt Middle School in Rockford, Illinois. This middle school position included: teaching electronics, electricity, metals, plastics, sheet metal and small gasoline internal combustion engines.

When I arrived that Fall to teach, the shop was a disaster. They had taken about 12 feet off the length of the shop for a hallway to the band room. All the workbenches were disconnected and piled up in the middle of the floor. The first thing I did was to place the tables in strategic places around the room. When I started to reconnect the electrical power to each of the tables, they told me I had to get a union electrician from the school district. The school district did not want me doing my own wiring. I said, "Bullshit". I have to teach my class. Therefore I wired them myself. I also discovered the small Briggs & Straton engines, donated the previous years were laying in pieces and many of the parts were missing. I decided to have the boys bring in lawn mowers from home. We also went to junkyards and picked up small gasoline engines, that people had discarded and repair them. I soon discovered there wasn't any metal available for my sheet-metal classes or electrical devices or wire for the electrical classes. I went to the principal and he told me, "Just go to the junkyard and get tin cans".

Each of my classes had 30 students and I had only 16 textbooks. I put up with this for about six weeks. I went to the principal and told him to have somebody else in here next Monday. He tried to convince me to stay until the end of the semester and I refused. I thought leaving would ruin my chances of ever getting another teaching position. I accepted the possibility and left to join the work world.

After leaving teaching I had several jobs. I spent three months working for Thermal Fax doing service repair on the fax machines. I felt uncomfortable charging the customer so much for so little service. Most of the Thermal Fax customers signed up for a 90 day contract. The contract included maintenance every 30 days. Most of the maintenance only took me about 5 to 10 min., but I had to fake it to make it look like they were getting more for their money.

I left Thermal Fax and worked for Ingersoll's as a Scheduling Engineer. I really didn't fit in that job. I was supposed to calculate the number of hours it would take an engineer to complete a design of a section of a milling machine. I then would multiply the number of hours it took to complete the design by seven and this determined the cost to the customer. The engineers didn't appreciate someone telling them how long it should take them to engineer a drawing. Some of these engineers have been around for years. They knew how long it would take them. So they really didn't appreciate some young engineer telling them how long it should take.

From there I went to Beloit Corporation as a Drafting Engineer. They had high expectations for me. However, the environment was so dusty I left there after a few weeks. I was getting nosebleeds from the dryness of the air and dust.

I left after about two months and joined the Amerock Corporation. Amerock was located right in Rockford, so I didn't have far to travel. I also received $.90 more an hour. This also made it attractive. I was hired as a Visual Designer. I designed drawer pulls and cabinet hinges. I worked for Amerock approximately 2 years.

One day about mid summer, I received a call from the Superintendent of Boylan Central Catholic High School. He asked me if I would be interested in teaching Industrial Arts and coaching football. Wow! This was a stroke of luck. I never thought I would be able to teach again. One of the faculty members I had taught with told him about my predicament at Roosevelt Middle School. Knowing this, Father wondered if I would be interested and come over for an interview. I had an interview with the Superintendent and the Athletic Director. I was hired to teach Woodworking and be the Assistant football coach.

Once again I was short of the necessary equipment for teaching. The first year I was able to have Ingersoll's donate a radial arm saw and a pedestal grinder. The shop was equipped with a table saw and three wood lathes.

The second year I was able to have electricity brought to the work branches. In addition that year, Father allowed me to purchase and install a dust collection system. In the Spring of the second year, along with the Home Economics Department, we put on a show displaying all the projects our classes had made. I received several accolades by parents and staff on all the furniture we made.

Because the furniture was impressive, I was asked to interview with the Warden from the Illinois State Prison. Because of his connection with some of the people at Boylan, he was told about the furniture we constructed. The Warden took me through the prison and offered me the position for $600 a month plus housing.

I was to manage their Woodworking plant. It would have been a lucrative position in compared to what I was making. I didn't think I could deal with being frisked every day. It made me very uncomfortable. They had a very impressive shop. They made all the state furniture. It was a complete operation. Lumber came in one end and furniture went out of the other. He told me the inmates working in the factory were the ones on good behavior. They made $.50 an hour. This gave them money to buy cigarettes and whatever else they needed. Apparently there was a waiting list to get into the factory.

I was at Boylan for three years, when a position opened up in the Public School System. They needed someone with a strong Industrial Arts background to teach at Lincoln Park Elementary School. They needed someone to prepare the children for the transfer to Wilson Middle School. Lincoln Park School was going to be closed the next year.

This was a very poor part of the district. The children there were primarily African American and streetwise. After teaching at Lincoln Park Elementary School it was an easy move to Wilson, not only did they have the equipment and materials for teaching machine shop but, the children knew me from Lincoln Park.

During the years while teaching at Boylan, Lincoln Park and Wilson I also worked on my Masters Degree in Industrial Arts. The Industrial Arts program was a major disappointment. I expected them to give me courses to make me more proficient. Besides writing a thesis and doing research, most of the classes were spent on the history of vocational education and the mechanics of writing a thesis.

Fortunately during the summer after one year of teaching at Wilson Junior High, I received a call from the Library Director at Platteville University. They were starting a Master's Degree program in Industrial Education and needed someone with a strong background in Industry. In order to be accredited, they needed to improve their library holdings in Industrial Education and Sciences. The University had just received a five-year Federal Grant for this purpose. The Director felt it would be more prudent to hire someone with a background in Industry then train the person in Library Science. Fortunately, I had just completed my first Master's Degree that summer. A Masters was required to teach at the University.

I met with the Library Director and the Dean of Industry. They were impressed with my knowledge. I started in the fall for $8300. When I started working, I felt like I was in a foreign land. Library wasn't a strong suit of mine. I had much to learn. The Library Director had remembered me as a student. I apparently fooled her even then. She was a tough person to work for. Everyone on campus knew it was Her way, or no way.

The following summer I started a Master's Degree program in Library and Information Science at the University of Wisconsin—Milwaukee. I completed my degree in three summers. My wife and children stayed at Lake Wisconsin. By having this as home base during the summer, cut my driving distance in half.

I was given the title of Divisional Librarian for the Applied Sciences. Agriculture, Physics, Chemistry, Math, Industrial Education and the Government Documents collection.

I started in the small Doudna Library. During the next three years a new library was built. This was to be called the Karrman Library. I was put in charge of moving all the collection from Doudna to the Karrman Library.

I got a print out from the Computer Center of all the classes with the number of students and the time they met. I then worked out a schedule for when they should come to the library and transfer books. In preparation for the transfer Paul marked out where the different collections were to go. I had the circulation department prepare the books in stacks. I thought it would take us a day and a half to move all the books. Some of the men students carried several books at once. Consequently, we moved the entire library of 500,000 books in six hours.

I never got any credit for how smooth the move went. The computer was given all the credit. This was typical of many of my accomplishments in life.

While at the University I participated on several committees, councils and the Senate. The University Rank, Salary and Tenure Council required being elected by the entire faculty. One year I was chairman. Many of my library colleagues became jealous because I was voted on the RST Council every year. I couldn't serve on the council the year I was up for a promotion.

I was always in trouble with the Administration. I've always spoken my mind, even if it countered the Administration's wishes. Students have always come first. An example: the Administration wanted students to build their own professional library. This meant the students would have to buy all of their books. At that time math and chemistry books were around $60 each. We were on a rental system, which was decidedly cheaper for the students. Therefore, I fought to keep the rental system, which they still have today.

There was a great deal of jealousy among women faculty and staff for my attention. It wasn't that I was handsome. It was because I was the manliest man in the library. Another reason for jealousy is there could only be one representative from the library, to serve on many of the commissions and councils.

My library position expanded over the years to include all Government Publications, shipping, circulation and facilities management. Facilities management included such things as: ordering equipment, shelving, audiovisual and a security system.

The Security System required installing a book detection system at the exits. Each book in the collection was inserted with a metal strip. The strip was activated and deactivated at the Circulation desk. This eliminated having a student check all the briefcases and purses for books and pamphlets. This also eliminated approximately 12 work-study students from circulation.

The Circulation Department included my secretary and 83 work-study students. My secretary scheduled all of the work-study students. She also let me know when I was in trouble with the other staff members. She was one of those people who new everything that was going on in the University and in town. This was very helpful in getting a heads up on what was brewing in the library.

I was also placed in charge of emergency preparedness for the library. My responsibility was to coordinate an evacuation with other departments and set up communications.

I was a professor at the University for 18 years. I decided it was time for me to join the real world. By going back into Industry, I could earn substantially more money.

I was offered a position with Barber Colman Company in Rockford. My position at Colman's was a Senior Training Engineer. At first it was like going back to college all over again. I had to learn how the various controls were operated for heating and air-conditioning. There were controls for electric, pneumatics and electronics.

My job required teaching engineers and service personnel how to install, maintain and service the different types of controls. The teaching was done primarily in the factory. We all flew to different parts of the United States and Canada putting on seminars. These seminars would last from one to three weeks depending on the types of controls.

Besides teaching, I would also solve problems for our techs, when teaching in the field. My last three years at Barber Colman's, I worked for the warehouse selling complementary equipment, not manufactured by Colman's. This usually required me working with the person on the phone and doing some engineering.

CHAPTER 7

MY HEALTH

In 1981 I was stricken with cancer. Prior to that my health was fairly good. I had a bout with ulcers prior to my cancer. The cancer was a different ballgame. One day I felt a soreness and swelling in my testicles. I didn't recognize it right away. My first indication was the sweating I had while teaching a college class. I noticed the swelling and soreness was getting worse. I went to my family doctor, to have it checked on. Up to that point I had been blaming my wife for buying my shorts too small. But as the pain increased in the scrotum, I thought I better go to the doctor and have it checked. As the doctor manipulated the scrotum he became suspicious. He contacted the urologist he knew at the Medical Clinic in Dubuque, Iowa. The receptionist replied, "The doctor doesn't have any immediate openings". Dr. Stussey was very persuasive and insisted she give me a time for an appointment in the morning, "I'm sending him down first thing in the morning ", he stated. The next morning I drove to Dubuque to see the urologist. As he was checking me he also became suspicious that it might be cancerous. In questioning whether or not it was cancer he called his partner in to look at it for a second opinion. They both decided they better put me in the hospital. The next day they scheduled me for a lymph angiogram.

The angiogram turned out to be an excruciating experience. There were two doctors working on me. They had a difficult time trying to find the extremely small gland. They made a small incision on the top of my right foot, in an attempt to locate the gland and insert the catheter. They tried for over two hours with no results. It was decided to try the same procedure on my left foot, with similar results. The doctors called a surgeon from Madison specializing in lymph angiogram. I was on the operating table for six hours. Lying on the operating table became very painful. The last four hours I had to urinate, but they couldn't let me get up to go. It was necessary to lie perfectly still. When they finally let me up to relieve myself I couldn't go. Apparently I had held back for such a long period the urine wouldn't release. They finally had to put in a catheter. Even after putting in the catheter I couldn't feel relief for about two hours.

After the doctors analyzed the results from the lymph angiogram their prognosis was surgery. They felt by removing one testicle the cancer would be localized. Surgery was performed the next morning. They use the same procedure as they would if removing a hernia. The prognosis after surgery was devastating. The doctors had hoped all the cancer had been removed. Unfortunately after further blood test they discover the cancer had spread through the entire lymph system.

The doctor said, "I hoped, by performing the surgery we would have removed all the cancer. Since this wasn't the case, I would like to send you to a doctor I know at the Mayo Clinic." He felt the Mayo Clinic had more experience in this type of cancer. He felt it would be prudent to send me there. He would like to send me to the Mayo Clinic to an urologist. The doctors at the Mayo Clinic deal with several cases of cancer everyday. The Dubuque Clinic only sees one or two cases a year. I decided to take his advice and go to the Mayo Clinic in Rochester, Minnesota. The doctor said he would try and get me in by the end of the week.

The urologist called the next morning and told me to be at the Mayo Clinic by nine o'clock Wednesday. My wife and I arrived at the Mayo Clinic Wednesday morning. We met with the urologist, who turned us over to an oncologist. He scheduled several panels. After the blood tests, we met with the Head of the Oncology Department, Dr. Hahn. They ran several additional blood panels and gave me a CAT Scan. Later that day, after the CT scan and additional blood tests, we met with Dr. Hahn and he went over the CT scan and the blood test with us. It indicated the cancer had invaded the entire lymph system, including my lungs. The doctor asked me, if I wanted to have the cancer treatment at Mayo's or go to Madison, Wisconsin for treatment. I said, "As long as I'm here, I might as well have the treatment here".

By 4 PM that afternoon, I was in the Methodist Hospital and they had started me on a regiment of chemo. It was unbelievable how sick I became from the chemo treatment. I felt like I was bringing up "mud" from 20 feet below the ground. I had a chicken dinner prior to the treatment. I never thought I would ever eat chicken again. I was one sick dude. I found out later they had given me a dosage at 125%. They put me on a constant drip 24 hours a day for five days.

After those five days, I was to return again in six weeks for additional treatment. Each time I went back to Mayo's, I went through the blood tests, CAT scan and would see the oncologist doctor. Then back to the hospital for treatment. This occurred four different weeks, each being six weeks apart. Each time I want back, I kept getting weaker and weaker to the point where I could barely walk. The cancer treatment caused me to lose all my hair, including eye brows and body hair.

After the protocol of four weeks of chemotherapy, Dr. Hahn would have me return every six weeks for follow-up tests. Unbeknown to us he was watching some very tiny spots on my lungs. About nine months after the original protocol of chemotherapy, we met with Dr. Hahn. When he started to tell us the results of the tests from that morning, he put his head down on his desk and said, "David, we hit you so hard with chemo. We thought for sure that we got all the cancer cells." He told us then that he had been watching six tiny spots on my lungs, and today they had multiplied to twelve. These spots or tumors were so small that only a CAT scan would show them.

He called in a thorax surgeon to discuss my CAT scan. Dr. Hahn thought maybe they could operate. The thorax surgeon said, "Let's wait another six weeks." When I went back after six weeks, they discussed my cancer again. The tumors had increased to over 40 in number. The thorax surgeon said surgery would be an exercise in futility. Because of the folds in the lungs he would never be able to find all of the tumors. Once again I was back in the hospital for five more chemotherapy treatments.

Dr. Hahn wasn't sure what chemo to use, because I had all of the bleomycin a human body could take. He said they had a new drug being used in Europe for the past five years and was available for trial at Mayo's. The drug is called VP 16 and has been used in Europe with some success. I decided what do I have to lose. I signed a form indicating it could lead to my death, but I felt I had no other choice. The protocol for this regimen was five weeks at five days each. There were multiple side effects from chemo.

My throat became extremely sore. It felt like I had swallowed broken glass. We tried everything to relieve the excruciating pain. I finally went to my local doctor, to see what he could come up with. He painted my throat with some medicine that he had in his medicine cabinet. The odor of the medicine smelled similar to the doctor's offices 30 years ago. Nothing that he tried worked on my throat. I had to constantly swallow to keep the pain tolerable.

One Sunday morning in church my chiropractor could see I was in a lot of pain. The next Monday my wife had an appointment with him for herself. He told her, "I could see David was in a lot of pain, Sunday." "Have him come over after work and I'll give him a treatment."

I went to see my chiropractor Monday evening. He said, "I'm not sure I can help you, but I'm going to try something. And you won't owe anything until you feel relief." After three treatments the pain was gone. I tried to pay him, but he wouldn't take any money.

Another side effect was I couldn't sleep. In fact I couldn't sleep for three full weeks. For some reason I felt if I laid down to sleep, I wouldn't wake up again. During those three weeks I painted the entire inside of our two-story home and constructed a large desk. I was like a human dynamo that just couldn't stop. It was making my wife nervous, because I just couldn't settle down. For some reason I just didn't get tired. I even went Coho fishing with my uncle at Algoma, Wisconsin for five days. By the way we caught our limit and had to come home.

After four years of going up to the Mayo Clinic every six months, Dr. Hahn said I was cured.

In approximately 1991 I begin having problems with my blood pressure. One day while spreading some wood chips around the trees I felt chest pains. When I would stop and rest the pain would go away. This kept up for an hour or so. I would rest and then spread more chips. Eventually the pain continued with out going away.

I had my wife take me to Emergency at Rockford Hospital. That night they put me in the hospital and the next morning put me through a series of tests. The radioactive dye indicated I had blocked arteries. The next day I was given an angiogram. They use a balloon type of catheter and pushed it through my arteries from the groin to my heart. In the area where my arteries were closed the doctor would expand the balloon on the end of the catheter to open the artery. I could feel the pressure each time he did that.

The doctor allowed me to go back to work after two weeks. Another three weeks went by and I had chest pains. Once again I went through the angiogram. This time he used more pressure on the balloon. I could feel the difference in the pressure from the first time. Apparently the doctor hadn't expanded the artery enough the first time he did it.

After approximately 3 years I was back in the hospital with more tests. Another angiogram was performed. The doctor indicated I had damaged approximately 17% of my heart muscle.

I continued with my work and retired at the age of 57. Due to the pressure at work, Darlene and I thought it would be best to retire early. We had bought a cottage on Buffalo Lake in Montello, Wisconsin two years prior. This Lake was located 50 miles north of Madison, Wisconsin. The lake was best known for it's northern pike. One of the problems we had at the lake was the seaweed. The seaweed made it difficult to swim or water ski. I did enjoy the lake for it's fishing and boating.

Darlene and I often went on pontoon rides. The pontoon was kept at the end of the pier. It was great to sit on and fish. I had a bass boat that I used for fishing out on the lake. It was a nice place for family and friends to visit.

We did a lot of work on the cottage. We added a great room and two new bedrooms. A Four Season room was added later. The cottage originally had a boiler system and we changed it over to forced air. New and additional picture windows were placed on the side and front giving us a panoramic view of the lake. Later on I added a 24 x 24 shop onto the garage for all my woodworking equipment. In addition I used the old picture windows from the cottage for Darlene's art room. The place had a gravel driveway and we had that black topped. I also added three waterfalls to improve the ambiance.

Besides doing all the improvements on the Lake property I also helped with several building activities at our church. One of the largest projects, I along with four other men from the church, was to remodel the gymnasium and change it into a Spiritual Center. Another large project was creating a Youth Center in the basement of the church. I also changed the exterior lighting for the church. The town of Montello had replaced all their streetlights to Early American fixtures. I put complementary lights around the church to match the fixtures down town. I also helped to renovate the storage room and change it into a shower room with three shower stalls. This was for religious conferences so the people participating could stay overnight in the church.

Another thing I got involved with was starting a Catholic Men's Club. I got the men involved in helping with the food pantry for the County. Every Wednesday morning we would unload a truck of food from Madison and distributed it later in the week. My wife also got involved with the distribution.

During Christmas and Thanksgiving, Brakebush Processing Company would donate chickens to be distributed at the pantry.

My wife and I also started a band. Joining us was Dan and Betty. These were the parents of Rudy. Remember the movie "Rudy"? Rudy was about the difficulties a young man had attempting to get on the Notre Dame football team. We started out with words on a sheet of paper with me playing a guitar. The girls were getting frustrated because I wasn't following the words on the sheets. I was singing the songs as I had always sung them. So to correct this I invested in a Karaoke and $700.00 worth of CDs along with several other pieces of equipment. We sang 3 to 4 times a week going to nursing homes. We never charged for our entertainment. I had always wanted to do something for others and this was my answer.

During 1999 I had chest pains, so Darlene drove me to St. Mary's Hospital in Madison. The doctors put me through the radioactive medicine to determine the condition of my arteries. They discovered there were several blockages. It was necessary for me to have open heart surgery. The doctor thought I would only need three bypasses, but I ended up with five.

When they brought me out of surgery they put me on a respirator. The tube they put down my esophagus made my throat extremely sore. I tried to get the nurse's attention, but she thought I was just hyper. She asked my wife "Is he always like this?"

For some reason it took me a long time to heal. My chest was sore for over six months. I went back to the surgeon to see why I had so much pain. The surgeon told me this happens in about 25% of the cases. Whenever my wife went over a bump on the road I had to squeeze the heart shaped pillow they gave me in the hospital. Once the pain was gone I was able to do normal work.

After surgery I had problems walking in cold weather. My chest would burn from the cold air entering my lungs. I always walked two to four miles everyday. Some days I had to cut my walking short because of the pain.

It took my doctor several months before he got my medicine right. Some of the medication caused several side effects. It became a process of elimination and adjustment of amounts. Over the years it has taken four different doctors to tweak my medications.

After we moved to La Crosse, Wisconsin I had a knee replaced. It has been approximately 7 years since I had it done. I have been very disappointed with the surgery. It didn't eliminate the pain. Now because of poor circulation, I walk with a cane. My legs are always in a lot of pain. Some days are worse than others. This seems to depend on the weather on how much pain I have.

In addition to these problems I have had both carotid arteries scraped, been diagnosed with osteoarthritis, planter fascitis, neuropathy, gout and a problem with enough oxygen in my blood. When I am inside I use additional oxygen. Other than this I feel good. I am also in stage IV of the kidney disease. If this disease gets any worse, I will have to go on dialysis.

CHAPTER 8

LIVING IN LA CROSSE

One day we went for a boat ride on the Mississippi River with our children. While traveling down the river and gently bouncing over the waves, I turned to my wife and asked her why we were living in Montello. We have children and grandchildren living in and near La Crosse. It is so beautiful here with the water and the Minnesota hills. In addition to making several trips to La Crosse each year for the grandchildren's school activities, it only made sense to move to La Crosse. We decided that weekend we should sell our home in Montello and make the move.

We listed our home with a local realtor and began searching for a place in La Crosse. We were fortunate to locate a home under construction in Brice Prairie. Brice Prairie is a small community northwest of La Crosse. The house is on a 1-acre lot. Because the construction was in the beginning stages we were able to make alterations.

The builder was kind enough to let me move some of my equipment before the house was completed. Each weekend

I brought up lumber and machines. On the day we moved, I had several of my friends in Montello help me load an U-haul trailer and a borrowed truck from Tommy Bartlett's Water Show. Our son Troy drove the truck. Troy works for Bartlett's year around. Once we arrived in La Crosse our oldest son Dane and our son-in-law David helped unload the truck.

We began going to mass at St. Patrick's Church in Onalaska. After a few weeks we decided to join this church. We met with the Deacon to join. I mentioned some of the things that we had done at St. John's the Baptist Parish in Montello and how Darlene and I might be able to help with some of their activities at St. Patrick's. The Deacon really didn't seem to care about our abilities and seemed to be rather complacent. His attitude was people come and go and I am important. I attended a Knights of Columbus meeting and was disappointed in their lack of organization. They didn't have anything prepared to start the meeting. We sat there for approximately a half-hour before the meeting started. When I came home that night, I told my wife, "what a bummer."

Later that week I told Darlene let's try the Catholic Church in Holmen. On the way to church that Sunday I told Darlene if the church in Holmen wasn't any better than St. Patrick's, we might just become Lutherans. We were familiar with St. Paul's Lutheran Church in Onalaska. We had attended several times when we visited our children in Holmen. Our daughter Teresa and her husband are both Lutherans, so we would attend church with them.

As it is turned out when we entered St. Elizabeth's Ann Seton Catholic Church. We were greeted by Father Malin. Father welcomed us with open arms. We could see immediately that this was a very friendly church. Barb Brown was sitting in the same pew as us and introduced herself. Everyone held hands during the Lord's Prayer. When going to communion Father repeated our names and the names of everyone who took communion. He has a fabulous memory for remembering names. After mass we decide to stop in a small restaurant for breakfast. While waiting another couple from the church invited us to join them. This couple has become some of our best friends. Also through this couple we have met many new friends. They were both raised in this area and are related to or know everyone.

I also discovered in a very short period of time, that no matter what, I was going to get hugs from Sister Bridget. I wasn't used to getting hugs from anyone other than family and then on a limited basis. Now it seems like the natural thing to do. Also prior to taking communion everyone greets one another. This church has a completely different esprit de corps.

Darlene and I became involved with many of the church activities right away. We discovered in Montello when getting involved with the church we met many more people.

Father Malin had just built a new home. In fact, it has the same floor plan as ours. At one of the Sunday masses, Father asked for volunteers to help with landscaping at his new home. Darlene and I went over on the day they did the landscaping and help place landscape stone around the house. Father has never forgotten that help, he reminds us every now and then.

We continued our singing since moving to La Crosse. My wife and I continued singing at the nursing homes. We sang at nursing homes about 10 years, between Montello and La Crosse. Eventually, because of my health, I couldn't handle all the heavy equipment anymore, so we had to quit.

I haven't physically been able to do all the building and helping with the grounds at our present church, like I did at St. John the Baptists Church in Montello.

Our new home sits on a 1-acre lot. We established a lawn and planted several white pines including several types of fur trees. In addition I also built a pond with a large waterfall. Every year I put several large chainsaw carvings of pelicans, hawks and eagles around the pond and yard.

In addition to our singing, my wife and I did various types of carvings. My wife does carving in the round. This is carving figurines (small statues). I do relief and chain saw carvings. Most of my carvings include eagles and bears. I have given many of my bear carvings to charity. I have also given away several of my relief carvings to family and friends.

I have had several people wanting me to make carvings for them but I denied them. I never wanted to make a business out of carving. I like to carve for the enjoyment. I don't want to be put under any pressure. I had enough of that when I was working.

Darlene was the first one to start carving in Montello. A friend of ours Helen had been carving for several years. Helen taught Darlene how to carve in the round. After I had seen some of Helen's carvings I said, "I can do that", she just laughed at me, like just try it, Buster. So I went home and carved a relief of a sailing ship. I have been carving from then on. I am still carving today, but mostly relief. I'm not as professional at carving as Helen, but I find it very rewarding.

Darlene on the other hand has improved over time and completes beautiful carvings. She does seem to be hung up on carving Santa Clauses. Many of her carvings have more detail than mine. She has a friend of hers that she is now teaching to carve.

I started chainsaw carving after I got to La Crosse. I had seen some chainsaw carvings in Duluth, Minnesota at a small shop and decided I would try my hand at carving a bear. My first bear turned out rather well, so I continued to carve with my chainsaws during the summer when the weather is above 40°. Of course I had to buy a special chainsaw for carving. The average chainsaw has what is known as a 3/8 pitch (this is the distance between each tooth of the chain) and I needed a quarter pitch chain. By having a closer pitch and a high-speed keeps the saw from jumping around. A carving saw has a tapered bar for making sharp curve cuts around the neck, arms and ears. The bar is called a dime bar because the radius of the tip is the same as a dime.

Fortunately a friend of mine has been cutting down trees over the years. He has supplied me with logs. Some of the wood was not in the best condition, but I carved it anyway just to have the experience. Most of the wood used for relief carving is basswood. I have it shipped from northern Wisconsin because it is better quality.

One year at Christmas time I carved 10 bears for charity and friends. This was the first time that I ever carved that many of the same thing. Normally I like to do things different each time to keep my interest.

One of my most detailed carvings was a boat for our son Troy. This was a replica of a Mastercraft boat like they use in the Tommy Bartlett's Water Show. A friend of mine painted the name on the side of the boat.

One of the carvings that I receive complements on is the large eagle carved from an eight-foot stump which was formerly a giant willow tree. I also carved two eight-foot totem poles. They now reside at Wisconsin Dells.

We have been very fortunate since we have moved to La Crosse. We are close to our children and grandchildren. We have met several people who are now our good friends. We enjoy traveling to various places in Wisconsin and our border states. We, with another couple, started what we call "day trips." and now we have four couples that travel together. The additional couples decided we were having too much fun. They wanted to join us. This is a real pleasure for Darlene and I.

I do miss my friends in Montello. Periodically, we will travel to Montello to see Helen. While there we go to see other friends too.

CHAPTER 9

MY ADOPTED PARENTS

I don't pretend to be a psychologist. As I've gotten older I've had a chance to look back at my adopted parents, and try to understand what made them behave the way they did. When my parents decided to adopt a child my mother went through the Rockford Diocese Catholic Services. She had discussed an adoption with Father McNally from the Rockford Diocese about adopting a child. My mother Alice was having difficulties with my adopted father. Feeling her marriage was starting to fall apart, she felt that bringing a child into the family maybe things would improve. My mother had a terrible jealous streak. This caused a great deal of dissension between her and my adopted father.

My adopted father, as I indicated in earlier chapters, was a nice looking man. Consequently he received a great deal of attention from other women. This attention of course upset my adopted mother.

Both Harry and Alice liked to golf with friends and neighbors. It was at these outings that jealousy raised its ugly head. If only they had a child brought into the family this might mitigate the jealousy. Alice could concentrate on the new child rather than dwell on the competition.

Alice claimed Harry was the problem that they could not have any children of their own. It was very difficult to adopt a child back then. Only through Father McNally could my mother obtained the necessary contacts for a child adoption.

Because St. Vincent's Orphanage was part of the Rockford Diocese, Father McNally was able to obtain the necessary paperwork and contacts. Had it not been for Father McNally, I would have stayed in the orphanage until the age of 18.

I don't think Alice knew what she was getting into when she adopted a child. It seemed to have put an added strain on Alice. I know I was not the easiest child to rear. I had a lot of energy and I always seem to be doing the wrong thing, consequently I would get regular spankings.

I believe I was in my 70's when my aunt talked to me about how Alice was raised. Apparently her mother used to give her some terrific beatings. This was probably where my mother got her child rearing skills. Beatings and threats seem to be the only way she knew to discipline her child. I have often heard it said, that you are a product of your environment. I guess that was true in her case. She never used a belt, but there always seemed to be a yardstick or broom handle available for the task of straightening me out, or modifying my behavior. I recall being a good little boy for a week or two. Then I'd be back in trouble again.

Anything that Alice decided I should do, would be self-serving and in her own interests. I never could do the things I wanted to do, such as learn how to play a guitar. For some reason she never liked string instruments. Harry tried to learn the ukulele one time and she broke it, out of pure meanness, while he was at work. I wondered why he chose to play a ukulele. But back in the 1930's and 40's when you went to football games, the ukulele and a heavy fur coat was the attire for parties after the Notre Dame football games. I loved to sing country western songs and play the guitar. She wanted me to be another Benny Goodman and play the clarinet.

When my mother first adopted me, she had me take piano lessons. The lessons ceased when we moved to the farm. Mother felt driving 20 miles to Rockford for lessons was too far. She never attempted to look locally for a piano teacher.

My mother never had a good word to say about my aunts. My Aunt Anna and Aunt Camilla were both very nice ladies. I never understood why my mother's attitude towards them was so negative. My Aunt Anna was involved in the Rockford Women's Club, so she would appear in the society page periodically. This bugged the "hell" out of my mother. She really had nothing to be jealous about, because she was president of the Farm Bureau Organization and a Girl Scout leader.

Alice was a very smart woman and I think she felt she never took full advantage of her abilities. My grandfather remarked to me one time, "Your mother and dad's marriage was like hooking up a racehorse with a plug."

Harry was a very strong and an opinionated individual. He was one of those men that did not like most of the other ethnic groups. He didn't have anything good to say about Italians, Swedes, Jews, Poles, or African-Americans.

Harry was raised in Bartlesville, Oklahoma. His dad was a sheepherder. He said, "I can remember living in a shack with newspapers on the walls to help keep out the cold air." Dad said they also had a washtub hanging on the outside of the house like you see in the funny papers.

My Uncle Clifford (dad's younger brother) would tell me about dad's childhood. He told me that Dad only went through seventh grade at Lincoln Park School. Clifford told me, "Your dad liked to fight and that he had quick hands." I admired Uncle Clifford a great deal. He used to come down to the farm and repair things for Dad. I was always impressed with his toolbox. My dad always used tools, then left them lying all over the place. After seeing Uncle Clifford's toolbox, I knew that was how I was going to keep my tools.

I started my toolbox with a half-inch ratchet set and a pair of pliers. When my dad saw the set he just laughed at them. His idea of a wrench was a pair of pliers and a pipe wrench. I always had problems with repairing anything that dad had worked on, because he usually ruined the bolt heads by rounding them from the pliers or pipe wrench slipping.

Shortly before the depression Dad's family moved north to Rockford, Illinois. The depression had a profound affect on my dad. My dad and my Uncle Forrie would hop freight trains and ride from town to town looking for work. My

Uncle Forrie found work punching cows. Dad located work putting up steel silos. They both did several other jobs during the depression. It was hard times for everyone. My grandfather would help them out by giving them a hog periodically. He also allowed Dad to put in a garden on his property. Because my grandfather was so good to my parents, Dad didn't have any qualms about having my Aunt Diane stay with them after her mother died. Aunt Diane was mother's half sister.

After the depression my dad served an apprenticeship at Ingersoll and became a machinist. Dad was a machinist for 42 years, except for the year he was on the farm. Dad always made good money working 10 hour days and five hours on Saturdays. Any work over 40 hours was time and a half. So growing up, we never wanted for anything, except for the year Dad was on the farm, we struggled to make payments. This along with missing his friends drove him back to Ingersoll's.

Many people that experienced the depression were very conservative with their money. Dad never bought anything new. He would always try to use and reuse old lumber and fencing on the farm rather than buy new. He always bought used cars for going back and forth to work. He never bought new tires for the car. He always got recaps.

Harry could always see the things that he wanted. He was never understanding or sympathetic about the things that Mother or I or others wanted. For example, I wanted to go with the FFA on a camping trip. He would not let me go. He said, "That's just for kids." Yet when I look at old photographs, he was with a bunch of guys on a fishing trip. He didn't consider that kid stuff.

My mother was a "sly old fox". Mother knew when Dad needed money for another car or a fishing trip. She had better have it available for him. Essentially Mother knew how to play my dad.

Most of this book has been about how I was treated being reared by my adopted parents. As people they were friendly and accepted by others. It wasn't easy for my dad to talk to other people. He would usually just stand around until someone would come over and talk to him, at large gatherings, other than family.

When we would go out to eat with other people, which didn't happen very often, Dad would be the first one to reach into his pocket to pay for the bill. There were times when Dad actually acted civil to me, but that was rare. Our interaction became worse, when Mother wouldn't let him sell the farm. She felt if we went back to Rockford, I would just get in trouble, therefore I became the pawn that kept him there.

My dad never really changed his attitude towards me, until I went to college. Up to that point, I was the "dumbest" kid around. He did not think highly of me. All of our neighbors had a different opinion of me. Unfortunately, I was at college before he indicated any positive concern for me. I was the first one in our clan to ever go to college and finish. Not only did I finish college, but I also completed two additional degrees and became a Professor of Library and Information Science.

I taught seven years in high school including coaching football. Eighteen years at the University of College and Industry. I earned two Masters Degrees and ended my final thirteen years as a Senior Training Engineer at Barber Colman in Rockford.

During my summers, I made additional money doing electric work. In the evenings and weekends during my teaching years in high school and the university, I became a union electrician and worked for a moving company. The summer before I got married, I worked evenings operating a punch press for twelve hours a night and five hours on weekends. While teaching at the University I started my own electrical business. Summers are always a problem because you were unemployed. Teachers' salaries are pro-rated over twelve months, which substantially reduces your monthly income during the school year. Many teachers took on odd jobs to make up the difference in their income during summers. I was always fortunate that I could find work.

My dad would have been very happy to know that I ended up working in Industry in Rockford. Unfortunately, he passed away before I moved there in 1984.

When Darlene and I lived in Rockford the first time, I helped Dad build their house out of town. I did all the plumbing, put in the septic tank, dug the field lines, put in the electrical service, electrical wiring and put up the wallboard. The plumbing was most difficult because it had been soldered and all the joints had to be unsoldered and fabricated.

Back in 1952 my dad bought two lake lots near Merrimac, Wisconsin on Lake Wisconsin. I helped put up a small building. We called a cottage. Building these houses took a great deal of labor. Back then I didn't have any power tools, so all the digging, drilling and putting in a well was done by hand. Today I have all power tools, what a difference it makes when doing construction work.

I also built a seventy-two foot pier, because the water level went out gradually. We had to go out several feet, before the Lake dropped deep enough for a boat and motor. The bottom of the Lake near the shore was quite stony, so it was quite difficult to drive in wooden posts to support the pier. In the Fall, the pier had to be taken out because the ice flows would take it out or crush it. This meant early every Spring, my dad would expect me to get up to the Lake and put in the pier, so he could get out there fishing. Fishing was his main goal in life. As long as he could fish he was happy. He also loved to play cards. Dad especially loved to play 500 and pitch.

I haven't included my sister so far in this document. My adopted sister, Suzie is six years younger than me. I never had a whole lot of interaction with my sister. She has had an unfortunate life. She has been married twice. She attempted to go to school, but never finished. Suzie never completed any activities that she tried. Most of her difficulties in life were of her own doing. After I found my family, I explained to her how she might go about finding hers.

Suzie found her family about a year later. She discovered she had a brother and two sisters. Her mother was still living in the state of Oregon. Most of what she has told us about her family wasn't true. She has a tendency to embellish the truth, so it's hard to know what is true and what is not. It's my understanding that her sisters do not communicate with her. They found out what a "phony" she is.

When our dad passed away, my mother changed the will. Dad always said that everything would be 50-50, but my mother bought into my sister's lies. Mother felt Suzie was down and out, so Mother changed the will to where Suzie would get everything. Mother did state that each of her three grandchildren should receive a small monetary gift. Suzie always cried the blues to Mother and my mother would buy into it.

Suzie always blamed her husbands for their failed marriages and the difficulties they had. I knew both of her husbands quite well. They were hard-working and good men. Her first husband was a machinist and he also had his own coin collection business. Her second husband had his own resort in Paradise, Michigan. Suzie felt she was being abused because of the hard work of cleaning all the cottages. She would come to Rockford and tell my mother, how hard she had to work. Her husband wouldn't get her a decent car. She convinced my mother that life was hell for her in Paradise. My dad would turn over in his grave, if he knew what Mother had done when she changed the will.

I don't know what my sister is doing these days. I haven't spoken to her in over five years. We invited her to a Christmas dinner one year. She did come up and join us. She just wanted to see what I had for a home and I never heard from her again. Suzie always tried to down play what I have accomplished.

I have never cared for people that lie and you cannot trust. I put Suzie in that category. It's unfortunate that she behaves the way she does. Suzie has missed out on seeing our children and grandchildren grow up and be a functional part of our family.

Suzie now lives in the cottage on Lake Wisconsin next to our Aunt Diane. She is not married and lives with a boyfriend. It is my understanding that she has to continue working, because she has no savings. Suzie never worked very long at any one job, so there is very little Social Security.

I wished I had known the change in Dad's attitude when I started college. I now know, he would have given me money, if I needed it.

CHAPTER 10

MY BIOLOGICAL FAMILY

F inding my biological family was very emotional. I had thought about my mother for years. For some reason I knew her name was Mary. I had always prayed to the Virgin Mary as though she was my mother. I never could understand how my birth mother could abandon me. I always wondered how my life would've been with my biological mother.

It took several years for me to decide to find my mother. Everyone knows who their parents are and what they look like, I on the other hand was in the dark. This reality had been gnawing on me for several years. I made a feeble attempt to locate my mother back in the 70s. I didn't look in earnest until both of my adopted parents had passed, out of my respect for them. Even though my life with my adopted parents was difficult, I still had respect for them. One day in the fall of 1984 I contacted the Catholic Social Services. I had moved to Rockford for a position in Engineering, therefore it was easy for me to visit them. In order for Social Services to do research I had to give them money for their investigation. The first two years of the search they were unable to find anything on my biological family. Each year I would contact them to see if they had any results. Several years later they discovered I belonged to a family named Manning.

The problem in trying to locate an adopted child's family is all the records of the adoption are sealed and cannot be opened without the consent of the mother, father or the oldest living relative. Since I was born out of wedlock, my mother was the only one who could approve opening the records. Unfortunately she had passed away several years prior.

I contacted the State of Illinois and had my name put on the State Register. The State of Illinois will list your name on a register and make it available for any one trying to locate you. The State sent a three-page form with no guarantees anyone would be looking for me. The reason I contacted the State of Illinois, is because the records from the courthouse in Kane County, where I was born, were lost. The hospital where I was born was also gone.

I became quite frustrated with the legal system. By the time they located my mother, she had already passed away several years prior. Because of this the Catholic Services wouldn't give me any information. I felt this was totally ridiculous because I was now in my late 50s.

Fortunately as time went on, the records from Rockford Social Services were moved to Elgin, Illinois. The Elgin office confirmed that I was in an orphanage. Because of the adoption laws and the fact I was in an orphanage, they were allowed to give me the biological family information. The way the law is written the parents or the oldest living relative must be contacted, before I could be notified of their existence.

After they contacted the oldest living relative, they usually have to write a letter of confirmation. Confirmation is necessary to see if it would be all right for me to contact them. It turned out that my oldest brother Tim had much of the same disposition as I have. He said, "The hell with waiting and going back-and-forth with letters. Just give him a call."

I was surprised to find out that I had several siblings. I was not told by the Rockford Social Services, that I had several brothers and sisters.

After Tim was notified by phone, he was stymied for a whole day. His wife could not understand why he was so quiet and walked around with his head down. The next day he began to tell the family about the phone call. Jennie his wife said, he couldn't say enough, once he started talking about it. They were all surprised that I was a boy. The family knew Mother had a daughter born the same time Tim's wife Jennie had a baby daughter. My mother told the family the child had died at birth. They found out later the child had been adopted right from the hospital.

I, along with other family members, have tried to locate her. We know that she is living because the nurse that helped with her delivery knew she did not die at birth. Unfortunately this nurse has Alzheimer's disease and cannot remember the birth.

After Tim received the information and acknowledge that he had another brother, he called my home. My oldest son was the first member of my family to talk to him. Dane was at our house to answer the phone and visit me in the hospital. He told Tim that I was in the hospital with a heart attack. Tim got my room phone number at the hospital from our son.

When he contacted me he said, "This is your brother Tim." I was overwhelmed that someone from my birth family had finally reached me. We talked for approximately an hour. Tim invited me to Aurora to meet the rest of the family. He told me that two of our siblings had already died. I had a sister Patti that died from liver cancer and a brother Dan who died from a heart attack.

Approximately two weeks after I left the hospital my wife and I drove to Aurora, Illinois to meet the family. My sister Mary and my brothers Tim and Peter along with Tim's family were there to greet us.

We talked for two days filling each other in on our lives. As I sat there talking to them I couldn't believe this was really happening. I was impressed on how they received me and what nice people they were.

My sister Mary was very generous with her family pictures of mother and a recording she had made with mother at the age of 70. She also gave me some hand written letters from my mother that I treasure. The recording at least gave me the opportunity to hear my mother's voice. I can't really explain to you what an emotional feeling it is to hear your mother for the first time. To hear mother's voice and not having the opportunity to talk to her personally was gratifying. Mary and Tim drove me out to the cemetery were mother is buried.

I continued to work with the Catholic Social Service in Elgin, Illinois. They kept providing me with information as they continued their search in an attempt to find my lost sister. After several weeks when talking to them they told me that they had found additional brothers and sisters. I was shocked at this news. I already had found five of my brothers and sisters and now discovered there were more.

This time there wasn't the hassle I had contacting the other siblings. The first one I contacted was my brother in Reno, Nevada named Barry Redfield. At my first opportunity, I went to see Barry. It turns out he is a Security Guard at Hara's in Reno, Nevada. He had been a military policeman while in the Service. After leaving the Service he married a Japanese lady from California. Barry and his wife have two children a boy and a girl.

It was about a year later, Barry came to Aurora to meet me. He knew the other members of the family. Barry, at the age of six, was raised by Tim and Mary. Barry told me one time, that he wouldn't be alive had it not been for Mary's financial support and Tim taking him in to live with his family.

Prior to locating Nanette, the Catholic Social Services located my brother Frank in San Diego, California. Frank was not sure how he ended up in San Diego. He thought maybe his parents had moved there when he was about three years old. Everyone else stayed in the Aurora area, except for those that were adopted from the orphanage. Ending up in

San Diego, California was a guess on Frank's part. He wasn't sure at what age he had been adopted from the orphanage. Much of the information on the three children born out of wedlock is somewhat cloudy, since all the births were done surreptitiously.

I had hoped by the time Barry and Frank came to Aurora, I would have found the other sister, but this wasn't to be. Two weeks later the Catholic Social Services from Elgin located my sister Nanette. When I contacted Nanette it just happened to be on her 70th birthday. She couldn't believe it, when I told her this was her brother and she had other brothers and sisters.

When Nanette's adopted parents had passed away, she found her adoption papers and just threw them away. She was so upset her adopted parents never told her she was adopted. She had literally forgotten about the adoption papers. Apparently she wanted to put the adoption out of her mind. It was quite a shock for her to find out the truth.

Nanette lives in a small town called Elizabeth, Illinois near Galena, President Grant's hometown. Nanette has three children, two boys and a girl. Nanette lost her husband several years prior to me finding her. My brother Peter says "She looks just like our mother."

It's a shame I didn't know Nanette when I lived in Platteville, Wisconsin because she was only about 25 miles away. She knew several of the same faculty from the University. She said, she comes to Platteville quite often, so we probably crossed paths.

Tim being the oldest brother was sought after for advice by the rest of the family. Tim and his wife had four daughters and three sons. He had lost one son in a drowning accident at the age of 22.

Tim had shoulder surgery about a year after I met him. After the surgery his shoulder developed an infection that spread through his body. Also there were complications from his hepatitis disease. Tim was treated for an infection in an Aurora hospital. He had been there several weeks when his body, develop additional complications, as a result of his hepatitis disease. He kept getting worse, so his wife called us and asked if we could get him in to the Mayo Clinic. I'll have to thank my wife for accomplishing this task. She called our Oncologist at Mayo's and he was able to set everything up.

They flew Tim from Aurora to Rochester in a Medevac helicopter. Tim was at St. Mary's hospital for about a week, before I had a chance to go up and see him. He was very pleased with the care he received at St. Mary's. He said, "As soon as I arrived they had approximately nine doctors working on me." About two weeks later the doctors felt he was well enough to go home. He had lost weight and said, "I'm going to walk everyday to keep the weight off." He did know that he would have to be on dialysis from now on. His wife had made arrangements for dialysis, so it would be ready for him when he got home. On Wednesday of that week, Tim began to lose functions in his body and passed away the following Thursday. He was flown back to Aurora for burial.

The following information on the family was all obtained from our sister Mary. Fortunately my sister Mary is very particular. She gave me several pictures including a hand written document from my mother. I am deeply indebted to her for all the information she gave me.

My mother Mary Susanna May was born in Aurora, Illinois February 22, 1905. She was the daughter Domini May and Anna May nee Niersbach. Her parents were both born in Europe. Dominic May was born in Hollenric, Luxembourg and Anna Niersbach in Herforst, Prussia. Anna Niersbach's was a housemaid in Aurora at the time she met Dominic. They fell in love and were married in Annunciation Church in Aurora. Their marriage produced two children Mary Susanna, born in 1905 and Peter Dominic born on May 8, 1907. Mrs. Anna May died giving birth to Peter and the child also died.

When Mary May was about three years old she contacted eczema, which left her blind for a few years. As a youngster, her father Dominic carried her in his arms when he went out socially. When in the tavern, he would set her down in a nearby chair and watch over her. One day when Mary was about five years old, she call from her chair to her father, "Papa, I see you" from that day on, Mary's vision was miraculously restored.

When Mary was 17 she had planned to go to the Franciscan Convent in Milwaukee. About the same time she had decided to go to the convent she met Paul E. Manning at a dance in Pottawattamie Park in St. Charles, Illinois. They eventually were married at Sacred Heart Church in Aurora, Illinois on January 17, 1922. They had five children Tim, Mary, Peter,

Patti, and Dan. Paul Manning died May 31, 1933, leaving Mary a young widow with five children.

In May, 1941, Mary Manning married Harry Redfield in Champaign, Illinois. From that marriage Barry Redfield was born on September 21, 1942. Mary Redfield died in her home at Maple Terrace Apartments, in Aurora, Illinois on November 4, 1981, from complications following a heart attack suffered in August 19, 1981. She was 76 years old and had just returned from a trip to Reno, Nevada when she had her heart attack. She was there to visit her son Barry Redfield and his wife and her grandson Joe, who was born on November 30, 1971.

Tim Manning, was born on September 5, 1922. He graduated from East Aurora high school in 1944. Shortly after graduation he entered the United States Navy for four years. He was married to Jennie O'Rally on January 31, 1945 at Irene church in Warrenville, Illinois. Tim and his wife Jennie had seven children. They lost a son in 1969 from a drowning.

Tim supported his family working for a carpet installation company as a sales representative in Aurora, Illinois. Tim died on July 18, 1992.

Mary Manning, was born on June 17, 1924. Mary stayed single and helped raise her younger brother. She graduated from Madonna high school with high honors. She worked for various organizations they include: Kendrick and Lindbald optical company, Mutual of Omaha life insurance, Valley Chevrolet, Fox Valley agricultural services, the Servite Fathers for 13 years and The Chicago Tribune for 17 years.

She was responsible for all the Chicago Cubs publicity and distribution of scholarships.

Peter Manning, was born on January 24, 1926. He also graduated from East Aurora high school. Shortly after high school he enlisted in the Army and served four years. While in the service he became a sharpshooter so they assign him to a tank where he was a gunner. During World War II Peter was captured by the Germans and was placed in Moosburg prison camp for approximately 30 days before the Americans liberated him. Peter and Ora were married on April 12, 1948 at St. Peter's Catholic church in Montgomery Illinois. Peter adopted her two children. Peter and his wife Ora had four children of their own. Peter worked for the graphic arts plant in Chicago.

Patti Manning was born on February 22, 1928. Patti graduated from Madonna high school. She was married to John Charles, on November 30, 1947 in St. Mary's church, Aurora, Illinois. Patti and John had one child. Their son is a tenured professor at Lock Haven University in Pennsylvania. Patti died on April 19, 1975 at the age of 47 of liver cancer.

Dan Manning graduated from East Aurora high school. He enlisted in the Air Force and during his service he was sent to Japan to handle the Yen Budget since he was proficient in math. After he left the service he met Mary Beth Salbury and the two were married on June 21, 1958 at Redeemer Lutheran church in Aurora. He and Mary Beth had a home in Montgomery, Illinois. My mother lived with Dan and Mary Beth until Tim was able to find mother her own apartment in a Senior Citizens Government Housing. Dan was an excellent bowler he used his skills to teach young children how to bowl. He died of a heart attack on February 16, 1982 at a bowling banquet for the young children. Dan and Mary Beth had two children.

Finding that I had nine siblings was probably one of the greatest highlights of my life. This is only exceeded by my lovely wife (we have been married for 53 years) and our three children, grandchildren and great-grandchild. She has always been an inspiration to me.

My siblings are elated that I found them. They think I walk on water. In locating them I instantly had 57 more relatives. Having all these brothers and sisters was almost more than I could believe, but it was a wonderful feeling once they were discovered.

It's interesting how we could've been together for so many years and yet we only have each other for the last few years of our lives. They are a very loving family, so different than my adopted family. I suspect my overall attitude and disposition would have been much different had I been able to grow up with my real family.

We're fortunate that we have these last few years together. We can't make up for all of time we lost but we can enjoy the time we have left.

CHAPTER 11

SUMMING IT UP

Well there you have it, I attempted to sum up my life on these few short pages. I've had many highs and lows during my 73 years. Even though I had a great deal of difficulty growing up with my adopted parents I learned to grow up fast. Much was expected of me but the hard work toughened me up for real-life. I found myself so much more mature then other people attending college. College students didn't seem to have a clue on hard work or the worldly things around them.

When I attended college I really didn't know what I wanted for an occupation. Back when I was in high school and college we never had Guidance Counselors. I knew I didn't want to be in agriculture because I would probably end up on the farm. Without any help I knew I would be at least $60,000 in debt just to start out. The farm equipment my dad had was limited and mostly worthless. With my makeup I didn't feel I could handle such a debt, which would probably take me the rest of my life to payoff. I realized I had several opportunities to manage other farms but I wanted to do it on my own.

If I had gone farming I would have stayed with dairy and cash crop. Although milking cows ties you to the farm 24/7 you receive a monthly check which helps the cash flow.

While attending college you must take several credits of general requirements. It was during this time I decided I would like to be in Industrial Arts teacher. After completing college I did get a teaching position in Plainfield, Illinois. One problem with teaching it's only a 9 to 10 months job, so you're always looking for additional work during the summer when school is out. There were times I had three jobs besides teaching just to provide for my family.

While I was teaching I often thought about going into Industry. I always liked working with machines, so there were times when I felt I would love to be working in a factory or teaching in a Vocational school or college. The only problem with teaching in a Vocational School is you had to have three years of Industrial experience. I was fortunate however to become a member of the Platteville University faculty.

Living on a farm gave me experiences I never would've had in the city. There were many times I was envious of the kids in town because they could play and run around. I had to go home and do chores. I couldn't be involved in many of the after school activities. My involvement with sports was limited to football. Football practice got over in time for chores.

I was also very fortunate to meet my wife in college. We were married on August 29, 1959 in St. Mary's Church Platteville, Wisconsin. We raised three children Dane, Troy and Teresa. They are all married and very accomplished in their jobs. We have three grandsons Brandon, Chris and Gregory. Brandon and Chris are both married with wonderful wives. We also have one great-grandson.

It seems being in the teaching profession one becomes a migratory worker. I have moved several times throughout my career but we are now settled in La Crosse, Wisconsin. We live on a one acre plot of land in the country. with a ranch-style home and a three car garage that accommodates one car and construction equipment.

In the summer I place my chainsaw carvings of various birds and animals around a pond I put in. We also had a local contractor build on a four seasons room. My wife thoroughly enjoys this room. She has always enjoyed raising flowers and now she has a place to display them.

I guess regardless of my parents both biological and adopted, I made it through life. I have made it to the end of the trail with not too many scars.

I put off writing this book for sometime, now that it's completed I can take a deep breath and say the end.